Sun Death

By

Robert Michael

ISBN: 1-4107-3351-3 (e-book)
ISBN: 1-4107-3350-5 (Paperback)
ISBN: 1-4107-3349-1 (Dust Jacket)

This book is printed on acid free paper.

1stBooks – rev. 04/23/03

Chapter 1

The Mission

"Space Shuttle Endeavor, you're clear for liftoff. Good luck on your mission and God bless all of you...T-minus ten seconds..." Bert announced with much anticipation for the final countdown. This launch wouldn't be postponed due to another mechanical failure or maddening alarm going off; no weather delays. "...three...two... one...we have main engine ignition."

Bert had been calling liftoffs for over ten years, but each one was like his first. This mission, however, was extraordinary with all of the secretiveness surrounding it. The information available to him a decade ago, was no more. Ten years ago, he would have received a ten-page booklet containing everything from flight preparation to details of the mission. Now, in the new millennium, all Bert would receive was a two-page memorandum consisting of only "need to know" information and everything else he didn't need to know.

1

That's what his boss Bigelow, also known as "Big Freddie," told him a few weeks earlier.

It was very clear that this mission, scheduled for liftoff on Labor Day 2004, had a top-secret classification of the highest proportion. All personnel at Mission Control had top-secret clearance in regards to the shuttle's missions, but that had been changing. Bert wondered about the shift in policy and why information was being taken away from many staff members, but he couldn't get any answers.

For Pilot Jim Andrews, this was his twentieth liftoff in four years, but his crew wasn't quite as experienced. Co-pilot Sheila Perkins, who he had just started working with in January, was on her seventh liftoff, but the last six were simulated. The rest of the crew, of six, had a total of three real liftoffs under their belts. To Jim this wasn't just another liftoff; it was expressly stated that this mission was the first of bi-weekly missions to the space station. This crew included two Russian Cosmonaut engineers that were going up, but not returning to earth. That made three consecutive missions where Jim hadn't returned with his full crew. There was definitely something peculiar going on with the space station.

Jim's suspicions started about eight years ago when information was slowly being taken away from the pilots regarding flight mission directives and objectives to attain at the space station. He found it strange that this space station, which he learned of in 1995, was top-secret and unknown to society back on earth. He was told to "get the crew there, get them home, and don't ask questions." When Jim questioned his supervisor, he was told, "Son, even I don't know what's going on up there. But we get our paychecks to fly'em up there, get'em home, and keep our mouths shut. And that's just what we're gonna do, right son? Now get back to work before Big Freddie has both our asses!"

Jim's supervisor, Benny, also was his best friend. They had been palling around together for over twenty years and Jim had seen Benny's behavior, regarding the missions, slowly changing. Benny would change the subject when Jim wanted to discuss work and the changes going on. Jim would push Benny to get information, but Benny would always put up a wall without hesitation. The Saturday before the Labor Day mission, they were at a T-ball game with both of their families. Jim was asking and asking about the mission and

Benny finally grabbed Jim's arm, pulled him off to the side, and exclaimed, "Dammit Jim, don't you go nosin' around about these missions! I heard you've been askin' a lot of questions to other pilots and this shit is top-secret! No details can be revealed about any of the missions, so just shut up about it before you get both of our asses in a sling!"

"I know Benny, but we've been at NASA for twenty-two years and just between us, you know something weird is going on! The missions have increased from one every six months, to one every couple of weeks in the last five years...and people aren't coming back! There are rumors that at least one person has stayed up there from the last twenty-five missions! What in the hell is going on?"

"I'm telling you son, there's nothing going on up there. The government just really wants the space station to be operational by next year. I think The President just got a wild hair up his ass or something and decided he was going to be the first President up there...I don't know! But what I will tell you, is that you need to keep your mouth shut, cause National Security is at risk! We shouldn't even be having this conversation right now!"

"You gonna turn me in?" Jim said sarcastically.

"You know son, you'd be a lot better off if you'd just show up for work like the rest of us, keep your mouth shut, and do your job. Hey, Jr's up to bat! I can see you've been working on his swing. He's getting to be a real slugger!"

And so Benny ended it again. He was getting good at changing the subject and it sure annoyed the heck out of Jim. He had never seen Benny so livid and Jim knew that he was on to something.

Jim and Benny had been hanging around together since Gerald Ford was President and Jim knew when Benny was right and wrong. This time Benny was definitely right about Jim keeping his mouth shut; he decided to take his advice and keep quiet. His plan was to observe and listen, figuring he would eventually find out the truth. Jim decided to listen to Benny...for now.

Benny always called Jim "son" and it fit their relationship well. Jim and Benny both lost someone precious during the Vietnam War. Jim lost his dad, and Benny, his son. Once they met, it seemed literally like a match made in heaven. But over the last few years, Benny had been backing off with how close he would get with him and it made Jim wonder if it was business, personal, or both. Jim didn't mind taking orders from his best friend, but Benny made it too obvious to others at work that they were friends. Sometimes he would be too easy on Jim, other times too hard. Lately, he was always too hard on him.

As Space Shuttle Endeavor's crew left earth's atmosphere, everyone was stiff as a board. Everyone but Jim.

"Okay crew, loosen up! The worst of it's over. You can breathe now...you're alive back there, aren't you?" Jim turned his head as much as he could, "I have one simple rule on my missions: no heart attacks!"

They all laughed and most of the tension was gone until it was time to dock with the space station. As it came into view, none of the crew could believe the size of it. It was like something out of a movie. A small fortress, floating in space, twirling endlessly with no destination.

The space station had been under construction for decades and still wasn't finished. Three-fourths of it was lit up like a Christmas tree, each light representing a specific room. The rest of it was still shadowed in darkness and it stood out like that strand of lights, with the loose bulb you could never find. Throughout the last five years, Jim had witnessed major progress in the accomplishment of this vast project.

Each time Jim saw the space station, he couldn't help but remember the many science fiction movies he had watched over the years. It created delusions of robots floating around a space ship. Or people going mad in space. Or movies about aliens trying to inhabit the earth. He couldn't help but let his imagination get the best him, especially with all the secrecy around the space station and the crewmembers not returning home. His curiosity boiled more each time he saw the structure that had become known as *The Station*.

Jim knew as soon as they docked, most of the crew would be segregated from him and Sheila and they would be policed toward a designated area. There, they would be watched over like vultures to ensure they didn't wander anywhere they weren't supposed to.

Jim, and his co-pilot, always had small objectives to accomplish on each mission, but he preferred to call them chores; they were so small and insignificant that he knew their main purpose was to get the

4

crew to and from *The Station*. Jim wanted to tell Big Freddie not to patronize them with these petty tasks and give him some real responsibilities up there, but he knew that wouldn't be wise. Jim was smarter than that, and decided to do some investigating on the Labor Day mission. He had to find out exactly what was going on.

Jim already had dozens of clues that he wanted to follow up on, but his last mission was the most bizarre. Shortly after takeoff, a cabinet sprang open and dislodged one of the passenger's metal briefcases; it belonged to a Japanese scientist. It slowly flew through the gravity-free air and hit the ceiling. Some of the contents, which appeared to be metal vials, sprung wildly about the cabin, bouncing around like ping-pong balls. About forty-five minutes later, when the crew was able to get up and move around, Jim tried to help the scientist gather them all, but he could tell the man was extremely nervous and didn't want anyone else to touch them. As Jim would grab a vile, the scientist would move quickly to him and grab it. Jim wasn't a fool and tried to read the labels as he grabbed each one, but was quite perplexed afterwards. Each one had "DNA" and a name of a specific type of animal on them. They went from cows to monkeys, fish to birds, and many other species.

Then Jim saw a few vials with some eerie writing on them. "DNA-JFK. DNA-MLK. DNA-PRESIDENT." Jim tried to play it off as if he didn't read them, but the scientist peered into Jim's eyes to draw out any guilt; Jim held fast. When Jim asked the scientist what they were, he jokingly replied, "Well you know we're going to Noah's Ark and I need to take some animals with me…two of each you know." Then he got serious and said, "No, we just want to keep DNA of specific animals up there. In case, uh, you know, something happened to them or something and we needed to clone them. It's just one of those things the government is doing. It doesn't mean anything…it's probably just to waste some more taxpayer money or something."

The scientist was trying to act believable, but he wasn't fooling Jim. That was the icing on the cake for Jim. Something fishy was definitely going on and Jim wanted to get to the bottom of it. Jim never mentioned that story to Benny, as he thought it might get him into trouble. He knew he was about to get in too deep, and he didn't want his friend to go with him; he was flying solo on this one and would crash and burn alone if that was what it came to.

After that, Jim decided that the next time he was on *The Station*, he was going to try and slip away from the guard assigned to him and Sheila and go snooping around. He wasn't sure exactly how he was going to do it, but he would need Sheila's help. However, Jim wasn't sure how much he could trust her.

Sheila was a 32-year-old woman that always had to try to outdo the male astronauts. Or, at least, try and make them look bad, so she would shine. On several simulated missions, she had undermined Jim's authority and tried to convince Big Freddie that Jim had done something wrong, or that she would have done better, in the simulator. Jim was considered by all of his superiors to be "the best of the best" and her efforts landed short and after looking like an ass several times, she accepted defeat and moved on to new prey.

She moved on to the rookie astronauts and she was determined to show them she was ready for pilot. A perfect example was a few months earlier when several of the co-pilots were practicing simulated shuttle landings. NASA policy states that at least two other people on the mission are trained to land, and dock, the aircraft in the event that the pilot goes down. On one simulation, Sheila had brought the shuttle in too fast and high to normally make a sure landing. The computer does all of the configurations on wind, speed, trajectory and everything else it needs to calculate whether a landing is successful or disastrous. Finally, at the end of the simulation, the computer gives a numeric result, which is very indicative of real life landings.

Nobody knew how she pulled it off, but somehow Sheila, coming in too fast and high, landed the shuttle and scored a ninety-six out of one hundred. As she came out of the simulator, all of the support crew, which included several women, gave her high fives and the place was going nuts for about a minute; one would of thought she had just become the first woman to land on the moon.

Dave Shnelling, the co-pilot in the simulator, was very critical of Sheila during the landing, but had a blank look on his face coming out. Next it was Dave's turn and boy did he intend to outdo her.

Dave was a maverick. In the Navy, he flew the F-14, one of the top air-to-air combat aircraft on the face of the earth. When he was in a crowd, everyone knew that he was one of the best F-14 pilots on the planet; or at least he thought so. He had done his tour with the military and even went up against some Soviet Migs in the Gulf War, participated in the Fightertown, USA, and completed the "Top Gun" class as the best pilot. He even changed his call sign to Maverick from the classic movie. His cocky attitude turned many people off, but he was very good.

With her score, Sheila had actually broken the record for "the fastest airspeed, at one hundred meters during a successful landing" on that simulation and had unofficial bragging rights among the pilots. It wasn't official because her speed was outside the parameters of what NASA considered acceptable and against the proper landing procedures; so it wasn't something to brag about with her superiors. Never-the-less, she had bragging rights and Dave was about to try to claim them.

During his chance at the landing, he made a real fool of himself. He was pushing every maneuver past an acceptable level and every instrument into what was considered the red zone. He came in for the landing thirty mph faster than Sheila, who only broke the record by three-which was the home run record that would never be broken. The landing was a disaster and the computer calculated that not only had the entire crew been killed, but at the speed and trajectory he flew in at, there was a seventy-eight percent probability that some debris would have struck NASA employees as well as civilians less than one-quarter mile away. Needless to say, Dave was pulled into Big Freddie's office and ripped a new one.

Jim knew that Sheila wanted his job, so just how much he could trust her was unknown to him; he had to find out. They had conversed on several occasions about the missions and she expressed some dissatisfaction about how the whole information flow had just been cut off. She even expressed some suspicions about *The Station*. Even though this was going to be her first live mission, she used to get debriefed along with the other astronauts on all mission directives and actually get to watch different parts of the missions from the live-stream video room. It had been months since they got to watch live video of a mission, and it bothered her.

By the end of the summer, Jim and Sheila had logged over seven hundred hours of simulated flying together. He had spent more time with her over the last six months than with his own family. He had a very deep respect for her, but also knew that she wanted to be pilot, not co-pilot, so he had to be cautious. Over the last month, Jim had been talking with her more and more about *The Station* and she started sharing what she thought was going on up there, which boosted his confidence in her. She was dating a pilot who was sharing all kinds of classified information with her. He was telling her many things that didn't even cross her boyfriend's mind as being weird, or suspicious, but they did to her.

Finally, while on lunch a week before the Labor Day mission, as soon as Sheila mentioned *The Station*, Jim whispered, "Sheila, what I'm going to tell you is just between us and I'll deny it if it's repeated, but I really think something weird is going on up there. On that mission a month ago, the one with the Japanese scientist, a metal briefcase…," and he recapped the incident to her. Her mouth dropped as he mentioned DNA.

"Sheila, I think we need to snoop around and find out what's going on up there on the Labor Day mission," Jim's heart was pounding. She nodded and agreed to meet for dinner to discuss exactly how they were going to pull it off without jeopardizing their positions.

Jim had docked with *The Station* dozens of times. With all of the hard work and time Sheila had invested during the last six months, Jim decided she deserved the opportunity to dock the shuttle.

"Okay, Sheila…Endeavor is all yours. Give us a clean docking with *The Station*."

"What, I don't…um…are you…um," he caught her by surprise, "Commander, give her one-third reverse thrust on my command and keep an eye on starboard, looks like sixty degrees/ten meters per second descent. Okay, on my mark," sounding as though she had been doing live missions for years, which made Jim very proud.

He couldn't have docked with *The Station* any better and as they shut down Endeavor, they looked at each other like, *You sure you want to do this?* referring to the reconnaissance mission they had planned. They nodded to each other and they knew what they had to do. They had two objectives on the mission: first they had to find out what was going on at *The Station*, and second, and more importantly, they couldn't get caught. They knew that they would have several other opportunities to unravel the mystery and the right moment would arise if this wasn't it. But, if they got caught, more than just their jobs were at stake.

The rest of the crew, deplaned and were directed to go to the left as they entered *The Station*. Jim and Sheila gathered their briefcases, which contained spy gear, and were, of course, directed to go in the opposite direction. Normally they wouldn't be permitted to bring their personal cases in with them, but this mission required them to be there for a total of three days and two nights, so they had to bring clothes and other personal items for the voyage.

They walked for about five minutes before the guard showed them their quarters. Jim and Sheila had separate rooms with an adjoining door that could open without the guard seeing. The first thing Jim did was look around the room for cameras or any sign of recording devices without being too obvious. They had discussed during the planning that once inside they might not be able to talk at all, so they both knew exactly what the other was going to do and when. To their dismay, there were cameras in both rooms, but fortunately not in the bathrooms, which they would use to their advantage. The plan was for Jim to go into the restroom and see if he could access other parts of *The Station* through the ceiling. Sheila walked into Jim's room and turned on the television as he headed toward the bathroom to take a shower.

"I need a long, hot shower!" Jim said loudly for all to hear, "See if there is a game on or something while I clean up!"

Jim went into the bathroom, turned on the shower and as he stood on the toilet, he decided to relieve himself before going on a possibly long excursion. The night before, Jim had a horrible nightmare that he was crawling in the ceiling, from room to room at *The Station* and as he went over the Captain's room, he fell through the ceiling, landing on his desk, right in front of him. As he hit the desk he woke up, heart pounding, and yelled, "Oh my God," waking his wife, who was always nervous before his missions. Jim always had nightmares the week before a mission and she worried they were premonitions of what was to come.

The ceiling squares were about twenty-four inches across, which made it easy for him to fit through. Jim had to keep two things in mind: don't fall through the ceiling and don't make any noise while up there.

As he pulled himself up into the ceiling, he could see and feel the darkness that filled the crawling space; he needed a flashlight. Jim had brought a few things with him that would help him on his adventure. His bag contained a small flashlight, an old map of *The Station*, a camera, a piece of chalk and some various tools if needed. He would use the chalk to mark his way so he could return to his room. With flashlight in mouth, he started to move…where, he didn't know. The excitement of the journey outweighed the pain in his shins, as his skin dented to the shape of the beams he was moving between. He crawled for about five minutes until he heard some voices; it was time to rest. Jim peered through a small crack between two ceiling tiles. He was above two men, who appeared to be scientists, and they were in a laboratory. They were peering through a microscope, each taking his turn, then giving the other his opinion.

"I'm not quite sure why we are having a problem cloning this calf, the last three have gone off without a hitch," one stated.

The other one looked again through the microscope and then at a computer screen. Then back through the microscope and replied, "It appears as though the DNA strand is deteriorating, possibly due to being out in space…I don't know. We never ran into this back on earth. This is part of the DNA we brought up here. Let's get some new samples from the animals and use them. We need about ten more cows in the next month."

Jim thought, *Ten more cows? What for? What the hell is going on up here?* He decided to stay in this spot and eavesdrop for a while.

"Yeah, and then ten pigs next month," the man grabbed a calendar, "and then look, they have like ten of something scheduled every month…this is ridiculous! They should have just flown the animals up here or something. I don't see at all how *The Station* is going to be operational in less than two years with plant life, animal life…hell they don't even have the half acre ready for the pigs, cows and chickens yet."

"It'll be ready, just keep pecking away," the other man laughed, "Hey, no pun intended. Lighten up Al, you've been really in a shitty mood lately. What's up? At least our families and us have been chosen and won't perish with the rest of humanity back on earth." They both laughed.

Jim almost lost his dinner when he heard that. His heart was pounding, sweat beading up on his forehead like a cold beer on the Fourth of July. He tried to move, but his arms felt like iron. He thought, *What am I going to do? End of humanity? What does chosen mean? Are my family and I chosen?* Millions of thoughts were racing through his mind, but he had to make his way back; he hadn't prepared himself for something of this magnitude, and he didn't know what was he going to do. He thought, *Should I tell Sheila or should I keep quiet? What the fuck is going on?*

Before he knew it, he was back at the bathroom. He jumped in the shower, turned it to cold and just sat there, thinking. It had been about thirty minutes since he had gone into the bathroom and Jim figured he should join Sheila to avoid any suspicion if someone was watching the cameras. All he could think about was going home to his family and exactly how he was going to forget about this mess.

"Is everything okay in there Jim?" Sheila asked as Jim heard a knock on the door.

"Yeah, I'm coming out," Jim opened the door, drying his hair; towel draped around his waist.

He took two steps and looked up to see Sheila, the Captain, and the guard standing there. The Captain, who Jim had never met in person said, "You should have just done your job and kept your mouth shut." The guard pointed a gun at Jim.

Everything went black.

Chapter 2

My Great Career

As Mike sat across from his boss Brian, he wasn't quite sure what the conversation was going to entail, but he feared he was going to be offered a new assignment. He hadn't even finished his vacation yet, but Brian interrupted it to set up this emergency meeting. Mike worked for the United States Government on classified projects all over the world; he was a scientist. He had just completed his last contract a month earlier, which lasted six years, and required relocating his family to South America.

They had met at their usual restaurant, The Mandarin Cuisine. The Chinese food was phenomenal as well as the service. The owner had obviously taken much care and consideration when designing and building the restaurant, as there was no hint to it being in the U.S.; the music, lighting, the attire of the staff, were all perfect. He saw the calendar on the wall that said it was the year of the Dog; it was February, 1994.

As Mike scooped his Won-Ton soup into his mouth, he would occasionally look up to see Brian going over some paperwork-probably finalizing a few quirks with the contract. Mike savored each bite, as Chinese food was his second favorite, only to Mexican food.

"You know Mike, the soup is the appetizer. You're supposed to eat it first."

"I know, but it's always so God damned hot!"

"You're telling me. Last time we were here, the top of my mouth peeled off after eating it," Brian remembered.

"Well then, that's why I eat it last."

"Anyways...what do you think I'm going to talk to you about today?" Brian asked with a strange tone.

"Look Brian, if it's about me and your wife...I'm sorry, it was just a fling."

"That's funny, reeeeal funny...no seriously? Of course now that you and your family have had your vacation between contracts, it's time for a new offer."

"Well, we usually get two months off. It's only been a month, but what do you got for me?" Mike asked, not wanting to know; he wanted to enjoy the rest of his vacation.

"A contract in Nevada. Here's the catch, I can't tell you what it entails, only that you and your family will be in a secluded area for ten years with little to no outside contact during the contract. You will be allowed one supervised, two-week vacation per year. By supervised, I mean you will have a chaperone with you at all times."

"Ten years?"

"Yup."

"Why so long? That's ridiculous! I've never had a project that long," Mike didn't like the sound of it already.

"Trust me...when you get debriefed, you'll understand. This is a huge; it's a Class One project!"

"Class One? You've got to be kidding me?"

"Nope," Brian responded as if it wasn't a big deal.

"You're fucking with me...there's no way!"

"You don't understand. You could win the Nobel Peace Prize for this one."

Mike sat back in his chair. He had been waiting for a project of this magnitude his whole career, but he thought Brian might be lying; sugarcoating it so he would sign on the dotted line.

"What's going on? This is a first! It must be real top-secret or something. It's not in *The Area* is it?" Mike was referring to Area 51.

"All that I will say is that it's very possible."

"You guys have never held back information from me like this before. Even with the Asian Contract, you gave me a hint. Come on, your bluffing, you can tell me something about it…can't you?"

"Nope…sorry. I wish I could, but my hands are tied. What I will tell you is it will be triple the pay per year…three hundred and seventy-five thousand dollars! By the contracts end, you could retire."

"Yeah right, don't fuck with me like that! That's a lot of money to joke around about!"

"You think I'm messing with you?" Brian pulled out a file folder, "Look, it's the normal offer letter. It's all here in black and white…read it and sign the last page."

As Mike read it, he couldn't believe how much they were offering him. Something told him that there had to be a catch, and not to sign it, but the idea of retiring in ten years was very appealing.

"What's going on with your hair Mike…did you bleach it?" Mike normally had dark brown hair, but it was lighter, especially the ends.

"No, we've been spending every day at the beach, and with the salt water…"

"Yeah, you're tan as hell! You're going to get skin cancer some day."

"Don't count on it, I'm an eighth Indian, you know?"

"What tribe?" Brian responded, not believing Mike.

"I don't know, somewhere in southern Michigan. My grandma told me years ago, but I can't remember. Now with her stroke she can't even talk, if I did ask her again."

"I guess I can see a little Indian in you, with the high cheek bones and all, but that's it. Other than that, you look like the average Joe."

"Brian, don't hate me cause I'm beautiful."

"Don't worry, that's not why I hate you," they both laughed. Mike continued to review the offer.

Mike always loved the "don't hate me cause I'm beautiful" line because it was his way of stroking himself. He grew up with a single mother, they were dirt poor, and he was always the skinniest kid on the block. He never had any friends-not because he didn't want any, but because they were always moving. He never asked his mother why they moved so much, but he figured they were probably being evicted for not paying the bills. The only thing Mike had as a kid was his pretty face; no muscles, no charisma, just good looks. He looked average to himself, but others would always compliment. Brown hair and dark brown eyes weren't attractive to him, but after so many compliments, he started to believe. So with all of his insecurities, he had one thing to brag about.

"You know I have to talk this over with Jessica," Mike responded.

"Yeah, you have twenty-four hours…you know how to reach me."

Brian slapped down forty dollars, grabbed his fortune cookie, and walked out of the restaurant. Mike decided that if his cookie had a positive fortune, he would take the project, but if it didn't, he knew he would still think about it. It read *Give the person next to you a big kiss*- it wasn't any help at all.

To all of his friends and family, it appeared that things were going great for Mike Collins, but they weren't. They saw a forty-two year old, successful scientist that did classified work for the government, and appeared to have everything in life. He had the nicest house on the block, though not living there for years at a time. He had nicer cars than all of his friends and family, though hardly ever using them. Moreover, he and his wife always appeared to be happy and content. The perception was very different from reality.

Mike made great money and they spent it like it was going out of style; especially his wife, Jessica. He had status at work and that made him feel powerful, but they didn't have the joys that a normal family had. Mike worked long, hard hours and there was little family time when they were on projects. Mike had promised Jessica that if he took another contract with the government, he would take the weekends off. On past projects, he could have had the weekends off, but declined to take them, which perturbed Jessica. Mike was a family man, and adored his wife, but had become obsessed with work. He decided it was time to change if he wanted to salvage his marriage.

Mike graduated at the top of his class at Yale in 1972 and almost immediately started working with the government on different classified projects. At first, he was more like an intern, doing all of the busy work for the scientists, never getting the credit he deserved. He would never be told why he was doing something, just to do it; that was his job. The government tested him for five long years before being promoted. At first, the government gave him small, very effortless projects to see how he would handle them. As he proved himself, he was given more responsibility, and along with it, more stress.

It was obvious that Brian really wanted him to take the job at *The Area*. But it really bothered Mike that Brian couldn't tell him exactly what the job was; he didn't tell him anything. He wasn't sure if Jessica would consider being segregated from society for that long. Mike didn't know how Jessica would react when he told her, but trying to convince her to live in the middle of the desert, with no interactions with society for ten years, wouldn't be an easy task.

Something really intrigued Mike about the job offer though. He loved working for the government and enjoyed working on classified projects. He had no problem not being able to tell Jessica about what he was doing at the office and even enjoyed saying, "Honey, I would tell you, but I'd have to kill you." She knew he would never tell her what project he was working on, or about most of what went on at work, but she would still ask, hoping that he would someday give her an insight. She was very pleased with the six-figure income and decided early on to just deal with it and enjoy the money.

This had been the first time, since starting with the government, that they didn't tell Mike what the new project entailed; that was what had him hooked. He knew this project had to be the most classified of classified for them to make him decide without telling him anything. He had made up his mind, but the key was to convince Jessica that it was the right thing to do for the family. His selling tool was their retirement when the project would be over, but he knew that wouldn't be enough.

Mike decided to do some bargaining and he would need to bring out the big guns for this one. Jessica had been bugging him for the last two years to try to have another child and Mike had stood his ground. She wanted a little girl to complete the family, but he was happy with just one boy. Their son, Billy was a real hellion growing up and that pretty much turned Mike off on having more kids, but now he wanted something. He knew he was a real jerk for using it to his advantage, but he was pretty sure it would work, and it did. Neither one of them knew what they were getting into.

Getting moved to *The Area* from California was the easy part. Anytime Mike had a project in the U.S., they would take most of their furniture and belongings with them. There was no need for them to do that on this project, as the house they were moving into was already furnished. All they would have to take is their clothing and some personal knick-knacks that would make them feel more at home. The government paid for everything, including movers, who did ninety-nine percent of the work.

Jessica had been through this a half-dozen times in the past and her Achilles heel was the unpacking. She hadn't worked a day since Billy was born, and her laziness showed. Sometimes it would be two months before the last of the boxes were unpacked. She told Mike that this time she would make a conscious effort to have everything unpacked by the end of the contract, knowing it was ten years away.

She gave the government credit; the house was beautiful. After Mike signed the contract, Brian gave him about a hundred pictures of the house that they were moving into, as well as the layout. It had everything a family could want, as it should considering it was their new world. It was five thousand square feet, two stories, had six bedrooms, four bathrooms, three fireplaces, a pool, Jacuzzi, theatre room, exercise room, two tennis courts and the amenities went on and on.

They had a staff of four to help them-a maid, a groundskeeper, a teacher and a personal guard assigned to them. The nice part was that the staff lived in the fifteen hundred square foot guesthouse out back. Each one of the staff had been at the house for over ten years and was excited to see the Collins family get moved in.

However, nobody was as excited as Mike, who would find out very shortly what his contract entailed. He had an unusual feeling about the project, but couldn't put his finger on it. He had never been scared of being debriefed on a project until now; butterflies swarmed the inside of his belly.

Mike figured that it had something to do with UFO's. He was an astronomy major and knew everything there was to know about space, the universe, and the planets. But over the last few years, he was getting some weird projects in regards to trying to contact life outside of earth. He was sure this contract was along similar lines and he thought he would finally get an answer to the question, "What is Area 51?" Brian and him had a lunch meeting at one o'clock, the day after they moved in, and he would be debriefed on everything then.

"I'm so glad we have an exercise room, my ass is getting huge," Jessica was looking at her butt in the bathroom mirror. She was wearing pink spandex and that was Mike's weakness.

"You shouldn't be wearing that, you know what it does to me," he walked up behind her, gently sliding his hand down her body from her breast to her ass.

The spandex hugged her body like white on rice; Mike loved spandex. He often bragged that spandex was his favorite and how he would rather see a woman in spandex than naked; probably because he could see every curve and crevice, but it left just a little mystery. He joked that if he was ever to be reincarnated, he wanted to be reincarnated as spandex. But he knew that with all of the sins he had committed during his life, he would end up on the rear end of some three hundred pound lady doing aerobics.

"Stop it, the movers are all over the house," she ended his fantasy quicker than it had started, "Do you think my ass is big?" She asked, knowing how he would answer, if he was smart, but she still wanted to hear it.

"Of course not. You know you're hot!"

"Yeah right, don't exaggerate. You just want to get some tonight."

"Well, I do want to get some, but that has nothing to do with it. Look at yourself," Mike grabbed her shoulders from behind, standing her up straight, then he put his face next to hers; they looked in the mirror together. "Look, you're beautiful. Look at that body!"

Mike was looking in the mirror at a five-foot eight, one hundred and ten pound blonde, with blue eyes; hair down to her butt. She could have been a super model if she was just a few inches taller; she was everything a man wanted in a woman physically. Her size-B breasts, Mike had surgically enlarged, per her request, to a large C

18

cup. He was happy with them before, but she wasn't and they definitely could afford it. She never worked out, but her body looked as though she did a rigorous three-hour workout daily. She was lucky, it just came natural to her; her mother was very thin, never gaining a pound though having four children-Jessica would never have to worry about being obese.

"Yeah, but look at this," she turned sideways grabbing the area just under her butt, "its flabby!"

"You want to see flabby," Mike took his shirt off exposing his out-of-shape body, "Look at this," he grabbed his belly with both hands, jiggling it like a bowl of gelatin. "See it jiggle, see it wiggle!" he sang, imitating the gelatin commercial he grew up on.

"You're an idiot," Jessica responded with a smile on her face.

Mike loved to make people laugh, even at his own expense. His body had slowly gotten out of shape over the years. He was a five-foot six, ninety-eight pound freshmen in High School who had transformed into a six-foot one, two hundred pound man in over twenty years. He was in decent shape other than his belly and love handles, which he was self-conscious of. His body was late maturing and that's part of why he grew up so insecure.

The doorbell rang.

"Bet that's Brian, gotta go," Mike kissed her on the cheek and ran out of the bathroom. He was so excited to finally find out what the project was all about.

"Hey, don't forget your shirt, dufuss!"

"Thanks," Mike ran back in and grabbed it…then ran out.

As he sat down with Brian in his new office, Mike felt very uptight; the meeting appeared to be more formal than usual. He sensed that Brian was very nervous and uptight about what they were about to talk about. Brian gave Mike a folder that read, *1994-The Collin's Project*.

"What's going on Brian, you seem tense?"

"Mike, I don't have to tell you that this is an extremely confidential conversation, and of course, nothing we discuss can be talked about with Jessica or Billy, but I guess I just did. Anyways, this house has been here for over twenty years, and it has been used by scientists the whole time for various projects. As you already know, you can't have any visitors and you can leave on one, two-week vacation per year with a government escort, which will be Matthew Fisher, the guard assigned to this unit. I'll introduce you to him after our meeting. Mary will be your housekeeper and cook. She does an excellent job and has been here for twelve years. She will take care of all cleaning of the interior of the house as well as the laundry and any cooking. She has a calendar in the kitchen of what will be prepared for each meal, each day, for two months out. If you guys have any special requests or want something changed, just talk with her, and she will do it. Groceries will be delivered, oh all of this is in the folder in front of you, feel free to follow along, sorry...I didn't mean to be rude." Mike opened the folder. "Anyways, groceries will be delivered on the second Monday of each month. You need to have any special requests to Mary by noon the Friday before, or they won't be able to process them in time. Pedro is in charge of all of the grounds maintenance as well as any inside maintenance that Mary can't handle. You have a teacher assigned to your family, Ms. Candle; she'll take care of Billy's schooling. She also will assist you with any personal or marriage counseling, as she has a degree in Psychology. Not saying that any of you would ever need it...we have just found her to be very helpful in the past."

"This reminds me of that movie, The Shining. He could have used her," Mike was trying to break the formality of the meeting. They both chuckled.

"I'm sure everything will be fine. Okay, if you have any type of security concerns, talk to Matthew immediately. He has an ample supply of weapons and technology to protect your family. Oh, and by the way, it's Matthew, not Matt. He hates to be called that." Mike nodded. "I would recommend that at some time, all of you familiarize yourselves with a few of the weapons, just in case. I'm not trying to scare you or anything, but you never know what kinds of psycho's are out there...just in case you would ever have to use them. Now, as you know you're inside *The Area,* near Area 51, so this should never be a problem. *The Area* is surrounded by barbed-wire fencing and I'm sure you'll hear the helicopters periodically flying around at night. They usually never get their lights on the property, but just remember if they do, they are there for your protection. Each morning, Monday through Friday, you will be picked up out front at eight a.m. sharp to take you to work. You should be home by six p.m. each night, barring any days that you get in the middle of something or decide to stay later. There are two Ford Explorers and two four-wheeler ATV's out in the large shed out back should…"

"I can read, come on, it's killing me, what's this project all about?" Mike slammed the file folder down on his desk.

"Okay…flip to the last tab in the folder," Mike picked it up, "Alright, it's not that big of a deal. What your job is, is to study the sun and use the parameters set forth on page fifteen of the section. There are approximately one hundred different questions that the government would like you to answer about the sun and other planets up in space. They won't tell me exactly what's going on-only that it is extremely important that you answer all of the questions and it will help with future space exploration of the universe."

"You mean to tell me that with all of the secretiveness about this project…you said, you couldn't tell me anything…and I'm just studying some planets?" Mike said in disbelief, "I know better than that. You guys know something! This is *The Area*! There's got to be more going on out here than studying planets!"

"Well first of all, it's not you guys, if somebody knows something, it's not me. Second of all, if you answer those questions, you'll see what they're looking for."

"Well, I'll tell you what, I was really stressed over this! I thought you guys were going to ask me to cure cancer or something with all of the money you're paying me."

"Don't be mistaken, Mike! This project is very, very important! I want you to understand that. We had a scientist on this for the last ten years, Dr. Sukami and well, he didn't quite cut it. He didn't get the answers the government was looking for, so he is no longer on the project! Look, I can tell you one thing…people's lives are in your hands! I can't tell you anything more than that! They need the answers and they want them like yesterday! It's not a difficult project, with all of your knowledge, but what's going to be difficult is getting the answers quickly."

"Wait a second, you just said you didn't know anything about the project. Now your saying people's lives are in my hands…"

21

"Mike, we've been through this before. I'm not supposed to tell you anything. You figure it out. That's your job! Anyways, back to Dr. Sukami."

"Will I have access to all of the data Dr. Sukami collected?"

"Of course, it's in the top drawer of your desk."

"If other scientists have been on this, why is it called *The Collin's Project*?"

"We just name it after whichever scientist is doing the current project. You know, it's a decade long contract…would you like to be working for ten years on the Sukami Project? Or the Wheaton Project?" Mike shook his head, "Exactly."

"Wow, Dr. Sukami! When they said he got a job for the government," as Mike opened the drawer, "I didn't think that he was in *The Area*. So what happened to him anyway…you guys ship him off to Timbuktu or something?"

"Well, I really can't discuss what happened to him, but lets just say, he's in a better place now."

"You make it sound like he's dead or something," Mike looked at Brian.

"You said it, not me."

Mike was flabbergasted by the indirect threat. Brian had never really pressured, and definitely never threatened Mike before. Whether he was imagining it, or not, it seemed as though he was being threatened now. He told himself he was just overreacting and to forget about it, and he did.

Brian left. It was onto the new life of living in *The Area* and studying the sun. Mike felt that he really needed to take what Brian said seriously. If there was that much secretiveness surrounding the project, there had to be more at stake than what he was divulging. He did say lives were at risk.

Mike knew that as soon as he talked with his wife, he would get the usual third degree. Questions like, "What is this project about or so what do *we* have to get accomplished to make them happy this time," would come up. Jessica always liked to use the word "we" like she had a mouse in her pocket. What Mike wanted to tell her was, "There is no *we*, I'm the one who does all of the work, brings home all of the money, and deals with all of the stress! So if I hear the word *we* again when we're referring to *my* work, I'll assume that you're speaking French!" But he was a good husband, never raising his voice and always trying to please Jessica and would never, never actually say something like that to her.

It was Friday and he had two days to get acclimated to the new surroundings and get settled in before heading to work Monday. Brian had introduced them to Matthew, not Matt, and he was a strange fellow. He was a huge man, maybe six foot five and two hundred and seventy pounds. Mike could tell he definitely lifted weights daily, and if he missed a day, at least thought about it. He said he was an ex-Navy Seal who had gotten a bad rap during his tour, but he really couldn't talk about it. Mike accepted that, as there would be many things that he couldn't talk about with even his own family regarding his work.

Something was really bothering Mike. He thought, *Why make such a big deal about this project if it was just to study the sun? If that was the case, or if they were lying, they should have not made such a big deal about it so that Mike wouldn't be suspicious.* Maybe he was reading too far into it…or maybe he was reading it just right. Either way, he was going to work diligently to answer the hundred, or so, questions so that he could find out exactly what was going on. Those questions were the key, and to answer them would answer all of the questions regarding what they were calling *The Collin's Project.*

Upon reading the questions, he could see that what the government was interested in had something to do with the source of the sun's heat and its expected longevity. Many of the questions were mathematical equations that the government wanted drawn up. Mike had always had an infatuation with the center of the universe, and that was his specialty; that was why he was here.

One of the first things a good scientist, following the work of another good scientist will do, is read all of his findings and a diary if applicable. There was no diary, which Mike found peculiar. Sukami and him had spent much time together in college, and Dr. Sukami actually got Mike on the "Scientists must have a diary to show people who follow, what his findings were," program. Mike didn't want to bring too much attention to his relationship with Dr. Sukami because he had learned over the years, while working for the government, that they only needed to know what was absolutely necessary. His opinion on that was solidified after an incident with Jessica's sister.

Five years earlier, Jessica's mom died of lung cancer and she was extremely depressed afterwards. Her sister, Jane, had come to stay with them for a while because she knew that Jessica and her mom were the closest in the family and her death was affecting her the most. One day over lunch, Mike was having a normal conversation with Brian about the whole ordeal and happened to mention that Jane's boyfriend was from Russia and was there visiting.

Mike didn't know that the information went from Mike's mouth, to Brian's ears…to Brian's mouth…to someone at The Bureau's ears. Then a tail was put out on her boyfriend; he was detained after a minor traffic violation. Someone from The Bureau, during the interrogation, slipped up and mentioned something about Jane's brother-in-law and that obviously gave it away. Mike and Jane's relationship had never been the same after that, because her boyfriend never came back to the U.S. Since then, Mike only answered direct questions and never offered information that wasn't specifically asked for by the government.

Mike and the family spent the weekend meeting the rest of the staff and familiarizing themselves with the property. Mike also unpacked his essentials, as he knew everything would be in boxes for several weeks, or longer. While lounging around the house Sunday, Mike was concerned with Billy's life as a young boy and the possible negative repercussions the contract would have on him. He was fourteen now and that meant that other than two weeks a year, Billy would have little to no contact with other kids his age. Ten years is a long time for an adult to have to do something like that, let alone a teenager. However, Billy would probably go off to college when he was eighteen so he would only have to deal with it for four years.

Tossing and turning all night, Mike couldn't get *The Collin's Project* out of his mind. He wondered about Dr. Sukami and where he was. He questioned, *Is he really dead? Or am I over-reacting? If I fail to get the results they want, what will happen to my family and me? Why is the sun's heat source so important? Whose lives depend on me?* His brain was on spin cycle and he didn't get a wink of sleep.

The relief of the morning arriving overpowered Mike's exhaustion. After a quick shower, he was eager to go, and could hardly wait for the Suburban to honk out front.

It was, as they always were, a black SUV, with limo tint all the way around that arrived precisely at eight o'clock. This was the vehicle of choice for the government and even in the movies. The twenty-minute drive to work wasn't the most scenic trip, as the whole area was desert, with little to look at; it gave Mike enough time to get his head into the right mindset. *The Collin's Project* was about to commence.

Chapter 3

Sukami's Journal

Four years into *The Collin's Project*, Mike wasn't happy with the progress of his research. He had asked Brian on several occasions about bringing in an additional scientist to help with the project, but it wasn't part of the agreement. The government asked him to take on this project because they knew that he could do it on his own. Mike wondered if he was meeting the government's expectations, since he wasn't getting any feedback...positive or negative.

Brian wasn't shy about addressing issues, so Mike assumed he was doing alright. In past projects, Brian would often point out opportunities where Mike could improve, but he lacked the people skills to do it tactfully. If it was the average person, they would be offended or upset with the way Brian talked to his subordinates, but Mike was used to it and secretly chuckled to himself when Brian got into one of his moods.

In four years Mike had answered about sixty percent of the necessary questions. Sixty percent and he had used only forty percent of the time; that looked good on paper, but as the questions progressed, they were increasingly more involved, so he knew time was of the essence. Early on, Mike decided to start with the hard questions and move his way back, to more easily pace himself, but Brian caught it the first day and corrected it immediately. Brian explained that in order to answer some of the more difficult questions, Mike would have to answer the easier ones and use that information later in the project. Mike wondered about the order of the questions and the rhyme and reason behind them. The answers appeared to be drawing a map of something, but Mike couldn't figure it out.

Mike still went home, night after night, with a feeling of dissatisfaction toward himself and the project, and he didn't know what to do. After devoting his whole life toward his family and his career, he didn't want it to end with a job not well done. Of course, the indirect threat, if that was what it was, always stayed in the back of his mind. It helped motivate him daily to try and be as successful as possible.

One night Mike came home and decided to put in a few hours in the library to try and conquer three questions that he was stuck on for the last four months. They were all related, and were noted as being able to be worked on simultaneously, so Mike did so. While looking through research book after research book in the library, he came upon a book that would change not only the project, but his life forever; he had found Dr. Sukami's Journal!

It was a grand sight. Here was a grown man jumping up and down like a little boy who just caught the final out of the Little League World Series. He wanted so badly to go and tell Jessica, but he knew this treasure had to be a secret; secret not only from his wife, but more importantly, Brian. Before anyone could know that it existed, he was determined to read it from cover to cover.

Another sleepless night passed, but this one was filled with excitement and not stress. He had developed some sleeping disorders over the past few years and it was starting to catch up with him. Mike wasn't tired tonight; he had to read until he found the answers, or found something to help him find the answers he was stuck on.

Over the first few years Sukami wrote in the journal, there wasn't any pertinent information to what Mike was looking for. Many of the concerns that Mike felt about the study were also expressed by Dr. Sukami. Sukami was also wondering where the research was heading and why it was so important to have these questions about the sun answered.

Mike had read the journal three nights straight and hadn't found anything of value. Mike wanted to know when Dr. Sukami stopped writing in the journal and thumbed to the back. It was about a month prior to Mike and his family moving into the house, which didn't coincide with what Brian had told him. Mike realized that he couldn't possibly read the whole journal within a few days so he selectively read portions. It would be two more nights before he would find what he was looking for:

> January 17, 1988—Have concluded that by my calculations the Sun will be struck by the white dwarf star at 3:24 p.m., on September 6 of the year 2005(+/- 22 hours). The fallout of the collision will be catastrophic. Although earth will survive the aftermath, the inhabitants will not. Sun Death will cause a thermonuclear explosion that will generate as much fusion energy, in one day, as the sun would normally give off over 100 million years. The oceans on earth will boil away and the atmosphere will be destroyed. All of humanity will perish. The heat and radioactivity will strike the eastern hemisphere, killing all life instantaneously. Life in the western hemisphere will be unlucky, as they will die much slower. The temperature on earth will rise a minimum of 75° (F) within an hour, eventually increasing to an unbearable level.

He had found the reason that the project was so important, but wished he hadn't. He panicked, thinking, *Was Dr. Sukami right? What should I do? Should I tell Jessica? What white dwarf star? Why haven't I uncovered it yet?* He wasn't sure about anything other than the fact that he needed to regain his composure for work the next day. He had to relax and not let this information affect his performance. He was determined to find out if Sukami was correct. Not only about what Sukami called *Sun Death*, but the timing of it. At any rate, he had about six years to figure it out and seven until Sukami predicted the white dwarf star would collide with the sun.

Over the next few nights, Mike was able to finish the journal and there were many other interesting points that he uncovered. The white dwarf was a super dense star that engulfs the mass of the sun, but is one hundred times smaller. When the white dwarf collides with the sun, Mike read that it would be like shooting a BB through a grapefruit. The white dwarf would be mostly unaffected by the collision, but the damage to the sun will be catastrophic and irreversible. Dr. Sukami estimated the speed of the dwarf to be traveling at six hundred kilometers a second and it would take approximately one hour to travel through the sun after it's initial penetration.

Within a few hours, the sun would blow itself apart releasing immeasurable amounts of energy and radiation. After the collision, the dwarf would continue on it's path, virtually unaffected by its violent collision with the center of the universe. With no gravitational pull from the sun, all of the planets would wander endlessly around the galaxy, eventually dying.

Mike also uncovered some interesting things about Sukami during the project. Six years earlier, while on his project, Dr. Sukami had a serious lull in his findings due to his attitude, drive and determination. He had mentioned several times that the government had made threats toward him, and his family's personal welfare, if certain goals weren't attained.

One morning Sukami awoke to the housekeeper screaming, only to find that their daughter, Jenny, was gone. The only clue left behind was a pool of blood out in the front driveway. After a month long investigation, the FBI concluded that Jenny had gotten up in the middle of the night, wandered out front, and must have been attacked by wild dogs or coyotes. The findings made absolutely no sense to Dr. Sukami because Jenny was petrified of being out in the dark and had been warned on many occasions of the dangers of the desert. The other red flag was that no one heard a thing; no screaming…no nothing. If Jenny had been attacked, there were six people on the grounds between the main and guesthouse. This devastated both of the Sukami's-there was no body…there was no closure.

After that incident, Dr. Sukami wrote in his journal that he really believed that the government had either killed Jenny, or staged her death to light a fire under him. Sukami believed the government did it so he would get the results they wanted. Throughout the rest of the journal, he portrayed a negative attitude toward Brian, and the government, but he was definitely starting to get back on track finding the answers they wanted.

This concerned Mike as he felt that Brian was making the same type of threats to him and his family. He wondered, *Were Jessica's and Billy's lives at risk if I don't get the results they want?* Mike knew he couldn't find the answer to that, but he knew that by reading the journal he could finally get past those questions he was stuck on. He needed to stay ahead of the game to avoid finding out. Mike knew he could make it happen, he just had to start thinking out of the box.

Several weeks later Mike was at a group of questions that were directed toward an area of the universe he had never previously been asked to look at. He had Dr. Sukami's results of the same questions available to him, but decided not to look at them prior to getting his own results. Mike was astounded; he had located the white dwarf star and it was traveling toward the sun. It couldn't be coincidental that they both came to the same conclusion. It appeared as though the world was going to end in the fall of 2005. Now that he had come to this point in the project, he could bring *Sun Death* up to Brian without arising suspicions about the journal.

Each Friday he had to fax updates to Brian. The information sent included what questions were currently unanswered and which ones were successfully answered that week. As he sent this fax, he knew he would be receiving a visit from Brian; Mike knew about *Sun Death*. The question was would Brian visit him at home during the weekend, or wait until Monday. He hoped for the latter of the two, but he figured he wouldn't be so lucky.

Sunday was another day in paradise for Mike and his family. They spent the day lounging around the huge diving pool, ironically enjoying the sun and grilling burgers.

Billy was almost eighteen and getting ready to head off to Yale to study science. Jessica was expecting now, as Mike had to fulfill his end of the bargain for moving the family to the middle of nowhere; he had put it off for four years. She was only two months pregnant, but was the type that was so self-conscious that she was already wearing a one-piece bathing suit. Mike figured that since Brian didn't stop by on Saturday, he was safe; surely Brian wouldn't stop by on a Sunday...or so he thought. All of the normalcy for the day came to an end when he heard a vehicle pull up out front.

Mike dried off and met Brian with a handshake.

"So what brings you all the way out here on Sunday?" Mike tried to act surprised.

"Mike, we need to talk."

"Let's go to the Library."

What was funny to Mike was that he was expecting the visit so he had played out in his mind how he was going to present himself to Brian. He had also made sure that the journal was in a safe place that couldn't be found.

"So what's up, Brian."

"Well, I reviewed your findings last night and it seems that you have just passed the half-way point. What I have to do once you've reached the middle of your project is sit down and make sure everything is going okay and let you know where you stand as far as your performance compared to what we are expecting out of you."

"Am I doing okay?"

"So far Mike, you are right on track as far as what we had projected. I'll be honest with you though, when I tell you that when I recommended you for this project, I did tell them that you would be a little ahead of schedule and that you were the best at what you do."

"Well I appreciate your confidence in me, and I hope that I'm not letting you down at all, but I really am doing the best that I can."

"Mike, don't get me wrong, I think your doing a bang-up job with the questions, but if you were doing all that you could, would you be grilling out burgers on Sunday, or would you be at the lab doing tests or at least examining figures in the office?"

Mike stood up, "You know what? I have moved my family all around this fucking world for you and the government, and put my wife and son through all of the bullshit that you guys make us put up with…and you want me to spend the only two days that I have with Jessica and Billy, working? I have spent my days off working on past projects, but I won't sacrifice my family anymore!" Mike was shouting.

"I'm not saying…"

"What you are saying is that everything that I have done to this point doesn't mean shit, and you're trying to put some sort of guilt-trip on me that I need to make you look good for your boss or something! I've been making you look good for over a decade and all you do is push and push for more. There is only so far that I will go to be successful and sacrificing my family is beyond that point!"

"Mike, you need to calm down! You have to understand that I'm just trying to get you to get more done. Look…I think your doing a bang-up job, between us…but that's just between us! What they expect out of me is to push and push just up until you're about to break, and then back off. Then I let you perform and then I do it all over again; that's part of managing people."

"Yeah, that's part of managing people, not leading them."

"Well, I'm just doing what I'm told, so don't get all bent out of shape about it! Just keep doing what your doing and everything will be fine."

"Brian, let's get down to the real reason you're here. You said this was just a project to study the sun, and by the calculations I came up with yesterday, umm." he was being sarcastic, "well…uh…oh yeah, that's right, I remember now, the world is going to end in the year 2005. What the hell is going on? How long have you known about this? I want some answers and I want them now! I deserve it with all of the bullshit I have put up with over the years!"

"Well, Mike, as you can see, the government has known for quite some time that the white dwarf will collide with the sun; we just have to keep confirming it. I mean, the dwarf isn't going to hit it head-on so maybe, over time, it will change direction and miss it. They have been doing studies similar to this since the early 1960's when they first got signs of this from the great Dr. Wheaton."

"So Wheaton was the first to uncover this?"

"Yeah, and boy was it a chore to keep it under wraps. He was one of the leading scientists in the country and when his wife found out…well, we had to…" Brian stopped talking.

"Had to what?"

"Well Mike, I don't want you to take this the wrong way, or as a threat or anything, but I'm sure you know that this can't get out to the public. The government won't let National Security be at risk…and we will do anything, and I mean anything, not to compromise this secret."

"Does that mean knocking off scientists if necessary?"

"Mike, I don't know why you would even ask such a question, you know I couldn't answer it, but we *will not* let National Security be at risk! If you want to read into it that we are knocking off scientists that aren't doing what we want, or talking too much, that's up to you, but let's be realistic here."

"I'm trying to be realistic, and I'm feeling a lot of heat from you to get results and I'm just trying to gauge what's going on here! I didn't sign on to something that would compromise my family or their lives!"

"You just need to keep doing what you are doing and everything will be just fine."

"So what's the government going to do about this?"

"There isn't much they can do! They can't replace the heat source, so the only alternative is to deal with it; try and survive the initial fallout and then survive without the sun."

"So how are the people on earth going to deal with it?"

"Well, I'm not sure exactly how *they* will deal with it, but I'm sure *they* won't have to for very long."

When Brian referred to the people on earth as "they," it stuck out like a sore thumb. It was as though he was excluding himself from the rest of humanity. It was as if he wasn't worried because he wasn't going to have to deal with it.

"So I guess *we* are all just going to die then…right?" Mike was prodding.

"Don't worry Mike, the government has a plan to take care of some of us."

"Some of us?"

"Yeah, and if you keep doing what your doing, and make sure your wife doesn't find out, or if by some chance she does, she doesn't tell anyone…you and your family will be taken care of also."

"In what way?"

"I really can't go into the whole plan, but let's just say that for the four of you, it won't be an issue."

"Is everyone going to be living underground or something…I'm a little confused?"

"Like I said, I really can't go into it, but get the project done on time, or preferably early, and you guys will be taken care of."

"Was Dr. Sukami taken care of?"

"That information is on a need to know basis and guess what?"

"Yeah, I know, why don't you think of something original…asshole."

On that note, Brian left and Mike was numb. He sat at his desk and thought, *What am I going to do? I have just confirmed that the world is going to end in seven years and that the government supposedly has some kind of plan that I can't know about to save me and my family, but only if I perform and fulfill what they want out of me?* He had to talk to someone, and it had to be Jessica. Mike knew he wasn't supposed to, but he felt like his head was going to explode; he had no one else to turn to.

As he sat down with his wife, he could see the tension in her eyes. Mike and Jessica didn't sit down and have serious conversations that often, so she knew when he said they needed to talk, something serious was going on.

"Mike…what's wrong, honey?"

"Well, I'm not sure exactly where to start. They told me that I was here to study the sun and its source of heat like I told you. And I told you that I thought it was kind of weird with all of the secretiveness around it when it didn't seem like such a big deal. Well that's because there is something very, very huge going on and now we're in the middle of it."

"What's going on?" she sat up.

"You're not going to believe this, but it's imperative that this stays between us. I shouldn't even be discussing this with you at all. I have done a pretty good job over the years of keeping the projects out of the family, I think."

"Honey, you haven't told me a peep about any of the projects since we have been together, so I just gave up after the third one."

"Let me finish. This is very difficult," he paused, heart pounding, "Okay, I'm just going to say it. A white dwarf star is going to collide with the sun in the fall of 2005, and all of humanity will probably die."

"You're not joking, are you?" she sat back, mouth open. She quickly covered it with her hands.

"Do you really think I would joke about something like this?"

She started to cry, "What are we going to do? The baby! We're bringing a life into this world...and Billy! We're all just going to die?"

"Well that's where things kind of get foggy. Brian said that if I get this project done on time, or early, we will be taken care of."

"Taken care of? How? What's their plan?"

"Well, he really can't tell me, but he said that the government has a plan and that some people will be taken care of."

"I don't like how you're saying that...taken care of. Are those the words that Brian used?"

"What do you mean...yeah that's what he said?"

"He didn't say some people will be saved or anything like that? I want to know how we are going to be taken care of! And stuff like, can Sis go too? When are you going to talk to him again? We need some answers!" she stood up, "we can't live the next seven years not knowing what's going on! I don't think I can live a week without knowing...this is going to drive me crazy!"

"Honey, I can't stress enough to you how important it is that you don't say anything to anybody! They'll probably fire me and who knows what would happen to all of us!"

"What would they do...kill us?" she asked.

"I'm not sure...exactly. But, remember the scientist who was here before us, Dr. Sukami, the one I went to college with? Brian insinuated that he may have been killed because he couldn't get this same project completed! These guys mean business and it wouldn't be hard for them to make us disappear out here in the middle of nowhere!"

"This is a bunch of shit! We need to get out of here while we can!"

"And go where?"

"I don't know, but away from these people!"

"These people are everywhere. They are the FBI, CIA, the law enforcement...they're everywhere. We couldn't get out of here...and if we did, we wouldn't get very far!"

"We could try! Come on, let's just leave...now, tonight," she grabbed Mike's hand.

"Honey, just relax, everything is going to be okay! I'm going to get the project done and we are going to be taken care of. I'm not sure exactly how, maybe we will have to live underground or something. Or maybe they have some complex, like a dome, being built to withstand the elements...I'm not sure. But it's better than being a fugitive from the government and trying to stay alive for the next seven years and then dying."

"Are you sure about this? Maybe you have made some sort of mistake, and it won't hit the sun! Is that possible?" she was looking for a glimmer of hope.

"Honey, they have known about this since the sixties, and I am the fourth scientist that has worked on the same project...and we have all come to the same conclusion half-way through. It's no coincidence!"

At that point, Jessica was getting hysterical and could hardly speak, "Well, I don't know, this is a huge fucking nightmare! I can't believe this is happening! I'm supposed to not talk to anyone about any of this now! I'm supposed to just bury this deep inside, and live life as though everything is just fine? My whole family, and yours, is just going to die, and we're just supposed to act as though everything is fine? I need a drink!"

"Honey, don't do that, it's going to be okay. You haven't had a drink in almost six years...don't ruin it now!"

"Ruin it! Ruin it! You sit there and have the nerve to tell me not to ruin it," she was yelling now, "This project just ruined everything! Our family's lives...our children's lives...and our lives! So don't tell *me*, not to ruin it!"

She barged out of his office and headed toward the kitchen. Mike was going to go after her, but he was sure she would stop herself. Jessica was a recovering alcoholic and it had been almost six, long years since she had touched the bottle. Moreover, she was pregnant.

While Mike was on a project in South America about ten years earlier, Jessica started drinking very heavily. She claimed that is was to escape from the reality of not having any friends or family in the area, and having to live in a part of the world that she couldn't even communicate with most of the people. Mike knew she had inherited it from her father, but was sympathetic with her. Mike was moving the family all over the world and they were putting up with all of the downsides of his career; he just kept quiet.

Jessica had a very forgettable childhood, never meeting her natural father. Her mother put up with an alcoholic husband that not only beat her, but the children as well. She never had the chance to ask her mother why she put the children and herself in that situation until a few days before her mother died. She didn't like the answer, but it gave her closure with her mother. She told Jessica that her stepfather was a good man for taking her and her four children in and supporting them until the day he died. She told Jessica that men like that only came along once in a lifetime and that a woman in her shoes would have to deal with the baggage that came along with it. Although Jessica didn't agree with her mother's logic, she kept her mouth shut due to the timing of the conversation.

That night, after finding out about *Sun Death,* Jessica drank until she passed out. It was her only way to cope with the turmoil she was feeling. Mike had a real problem now; he had just broken the first and most important rule of working on a top-secret project: Do not tell your spouse. He had a bad feeling about the future of *The Collin's Project.*

Chapter 4

The Ultimatum

It was Wednesday now, three days since Mike told his wife about *Sun Death* and things were starting to get back to normal at home…with the exception of Jessica's drinking. She was back on the daily drinking routine and it was affecting her motivation. Mike decided to let her go for a while and see if she would catch herself before she fell flat on her face, but he was very concerned about their unborn child. Concerned that the new life inside her, didn't even cross her mind. It was as though she was in shock or a deep trance.

It seemed to be just another day at the laboratory before Brian showed up and wanted to have another conversation with Mike. Mike was unsure of the nature of it, but knew it was serious because of Brian's facial expression; he wore his emotions on his face.

As they sat down in Mikes' office, Mike felt like he could slice the tension in the air with a knife. Brian just sat there for what seemed to be an eternity. He looked down, then up, then down again. After a few minutes, he sighed, eventually made eye contact with Mike, and spoke.

"Mike, I know you're going to be upset, but we know you told your wife about everything Sunday after I left."

"Bullshit! I didn't say anything to her."

"We know. Let's not make this anymore difficult than it needs to be."

"Look, I don't know what you're talking about, but…"

"Mike, your house is bugged! It's been bugged since the day it was built! Do you actually think we would let top-secret projects, that put National Security at risk, go unmonitored by us? Come on, wake up and smell the coffee!"

"So you guys have been spying on us? You have been invading our privacy? That's against the law without my knowing…this is ridiculous!"

"Mike, there are two ways this conversation can go…and so far, it's not going in the direction that will be most favorable for you."

"Here we go…more threats."

"Look, first of all, you have violated the contract that you signed with us. You were given specific instructions, on every project, that you can't discuss anything regarding the project with any family members. The only thing saving your ass is that Jessica specifically said, during your conversation, that you have never told her about any of your projects in the past. I had to really pull some strings…and take an ass chewing to get you to stay on this one!"

"So is this where I am supposed to thank you?"

"You know, we have to work together for many, many more years, so we really need to get on the same page and start working together. So, I have to ask you," he pulled out a form and a pen, "Do you feel that after giving your spouse the information that you did, that she can be relied upon to keep this information secret and not divulge it to anyone, including other family members?"

"Yes, I stressed the importance of that. And I will talk to her again tonight."

"Can the United States Government count on you, from this day and time going forward, that this sort of incident will never happen again?"

"Yes."

"I'll fill in the rest. This is just a formality that we have to do, especially on a project of this magnitude. I want you to understand the importance of this! There are probably people listening and even watching us right now!"

Mike looked around wandering if he has been on camera since the day he started and furthermore if there were cameras in his home. The thought made him furious.

"So there's some asshole somewhere, listening to me make love to my wife...probably jerking off, and I'm supposed to just go home and act normal...right?"

"Well I can understand that it's going to be awkward for a while, but I don't think you should tell Jessica! That would make this much more difficult."

"Oh, you can bet I won't! She's really taking this hard and I'm not sure exactly what is going to happen! She's drinking every day and she's still in shock over the whole thing!"

"That's very understandable, but I need to re-emphasize the importance of this project. I don't want you to take this the wrong way, but I have to tell you that we had similar problems on the Sukami Project and I don't want a similar ending. That reminds me, you mentioned to Jessica that you had came up with similar results as Sukami, how did you know that?"

"I just figured we had. We use many of the same principles and procedures in finding answers to these types of questions...and are both experts in the field," he had to think up something fast, "and when we had our conversation, you had mentioned that the findings were similar...I remember distinctly!" Brian couldn't know he found Sukami's journal...not yet.

"I don't remember that part of our conversation, but you haven't found anything of his? Like any notes, books or anything else, have you?"

"No...why?"

"We were just curious. Anyways, back to this project, I want you to know that these questions are extremely important to all of mankind! It's very possible that by completing this project on time, or early, you could be responsible for saving lives! Who knows, maybe even all of humanity! And please understand that it's imperative that this incident doesn't affect any aspect of the project. Remember that if you fulfill it, you and your family will be taken care of."

"I'm really not liking the way you keep saying that Brian. What do you mean taken care of? Is it just us four? What about my Mom?"

"They want me to be careful with how I word things because…well…it just sounds weird! What do you want me to say, your lives will be spared? We don't want people thinking that we're playing God or anything. It's easy…you do your job and you guys live. It's kind of like a job out in the real world; if you don't do your job, there's a consequence…you get fired! On this job, the consequence is much more severe, but it makes you think long and hard before making a poor decision."

"You say that they don't want to play God, but that is exactly what they're doing!"

"Call it what you want, but let's get back to your other question. I would just get it out of your mind about anybody else, other than your wife and children, being taken care of. Where we are all going, is a place that has limitations on how many people can go there…due to the resources available to keep them alive for an extended period of time. Look, I'm going into things that I really can't even discuss with you!"

"Well, don't worry about Jessica. I'll sit down with her tonight and make sure that all of this strictly stays between us. As far as the threats, I think you've made yourself very clear! It's very disheartening and unmotivating to get your life threatened so lets just assume that I understand that if I don't get this project completed, on or before the due date, we will perish with the rest of humanity! Otherwise, I'm going to say the same thing as you, I'm not threatening you, but a man can only let his family get threatened so many times before he has to do something about it!"

"I'm not sure exactly what you're getting at Mike?" Brian sat up in his seat.

"What I'm getting at, is that you can stop with the threats because they're not going to motivate me any more or make me produce any faster! It's just going to piss me off!"

"I just do what I'm told, so I guess if you produce, it won't be an issue."

With that comment, Brian left; he always had to have the last word. Mike wasn't sure exactly what to think after the conversation-he felt numb all over. There were hundreds of things going through his mind, and he couldn't process them quick enough to focus on one. He had to call it a day, so he called his driver and went home early.

It was rare for Mike to go home and want to drink, but this was one of those days. He kept a bottle of tequila in his office in the bottom drawer. He had been swigging on the same bottle for almost a year and a half, and it was still about one-quarter full. Every once in a while, after a really tough day at work, he would come home and just take a mouthful; only one. He always stopped at that point, as he usually had some sort of paperwork or something to do with work and he always saved his drinking for his days off. Jessica had bought him the bottle about two years earlier because he loved tequila and was fascinated after seeing this type that had a worm on the bottom of the bottle. Today was definitely a day that he would take a swig; maybe even two.

As Mike opened the front door to his house, he wondered what kind of condition Jessica would be in and what she had done all day. He was getting increasingly concerned with her drinking. She hadn't stayed dry for even a day since she learned of *Sun Death*.

As he walked into the house, he could hear that the television was very loud, which was peculiar. As he entered the living room, he could see Jessica passed out on the couch, bottle dangling half-in, half-out of her hand, slightly kissing the carpet. It wasn't even five in the evening and she was finished for the night. He walked over to her and lightly smacked her on the cheek, hoping to get a response-no luck. He turned off the television, took what was left of the whiskey, and poured it down the kitchen sink.

After taking a shot of tequila, which took the edge off considerably, he decided to go find Billy. As he walked up the stairs to his son's room, he couldn't help but be proud of his son and hope that Billy wasn't thinking his Mom was a bad person. He was eighteen years old and at the age where some of the kids were experimenting with alcohol and drugs. Billy had straight A's and hadn't shown any negative side affects from being secluded from society for an extended amount of time.

As Mike reached for Billy's door handle, he hoped to find him playing a video game or doing something relaxing; find him doing fun things that teenagers do. For the last year, Billy was one hundred percent devoted to studying all of his school subjects and was following in Mike's footsteps with his interest in science, especially outer space. Mike found it extremely odd that when he would ask Billy what type of videogames or other cool things he wanted, he would always ask for books or computer programs to enhance his knowledge. Sometimes it made Mike a little nervous that maybe his son was turning into a nerd and he would go ahead and buy him something fun or a cool. But Billy never was interested with those types of things.

Billy was the complete antithesis of Mike during his youth. Mike loved to screw around, ditch school, and cram before tests. He didn't need to study or have the drive or motivation to do it; his good grades just came naturally. Mike averaged a 4.0 throughout high school and college without even trying.

When Mike's parents would ask him what he wanted, he would ask for things like a new skateboard or some baseball cards, so he could chew the gum and put the cards in the spokes of his bike. Mike just worried that Billy would grow up with thick taped-up glasses or some high water, tight pants. He wanted Billy to be accepted by society as a normal person, but still be academically sound.

"Hey Billy, you in there?" Mike said as he lightly tapped on the door.

"Yeah, come on in. Just doing some sketches of the science project I am working on for the Science Fair. I really want to win."

"What is your project?"

"I am going to try and re-create a lunar eclipse, with a rotating earth…and show how the moon slides between the earth and the sun and creates it. It's going to be really informative. The only thing that stinks is I can't be there for the judging. I have to mail it in and wait for the results since we're in here. You know, Dad, when I grow up I want to be a famous scientist just like you, and work for the government on top-secret projects. It would be so interesting to tell your friends that you can't discuss your work because it's classified."

"Son, trust me, you don't want to work for the government. It's not all that it's cracked up to be. All of us sacrifice a lot for me to have a job like this. I can't just take you guys somewhere to have fun; my job dictates our whole lives. You don't want to live like this as a child and an adult." Now he was using child psychology, "I think it would be cooler to be an astronaut or a scientist for a big university or something! Who knows, maybe you could find the cure for Cancer or something! That would be cooler than my job!"

"Yeah, maybe your right."

"You know, your project sounds really cool. If you need any help, just let me know...by the way, what did you and Mom do today?"

"Well, after I was done with my schooling, I went for a swim and watched the Discovery channel. It was really cool...today they showed how the earth was one great, big continent at one time and how the continents were formed and..."

"That sounds really neat Billy, what was Mom doing all day?"

"Well I really didn't see her much, but she seemed to be acting really weird when I saw her this afternoon."

"Like what?" Mike knew what the answer was, but needed confirmation.

"I don't know, kinda weird...like when Uncle Jeff came over for that New Years party and was acting real goofy and walking funny and ended up sleeping in my bed all night. Yeah, that's kinda how she was acting. Why, is Mom okay?"

"Yeah, she's fine. She's just a little home sick right now, but she'll be fine."

"Okay...well, I better get back to my project."

"Well, I'm off to my office as usual for a few hours of paperwork. It's Mary's night off so the food is in the fridge when you're ready to eat. Just pop it in the microwave...oh, and I had her whip up some chocolate chip cookies for you, they're on the counter."

"Thanks Dad."

"Your welcome. Talk to you later."

Mike was off to the library to do some paperwork, which had become a nightly routine. He would put in ten hours at work, then another two at home, which left very little time for the family during the week. Mike was always avid about staying a family man and never letting work take over his life, but over the last ten years, he had let those morals slip away; at least he was taking weekends off this time. Mike really wanted to get this last project done and then retire. With the discoveries he had made on this project, his whole prospective on his family's future had changed.

Mike thought *If we're taken care of, what will happen to us?   I have about $500,000 saved up for retirement, not including my investments...should I withdraw it?   Will there even be a money system where we were going?*   There were so many unanswered questions and he could see why Jessica was on the edge.

Mike woke up in his office chair which astonished him; it was 2 a.m.   He rarely fell asleep in his chair, as it always put the worst crook in his back.   He decided to pick up Jessica on the way to bed.   He hoped that she had sobered up enough to actually make the trip up the flight of stairs on her own.   The sofa was vacant so he headed up to their room, but his bed was empty; so was Billy's.

Mike ran back to his room and out to the balcony-no sign of her, or Billy in the pool.   Then, as he peered out to the barn, where the Explorers were supposed to be, he had a sick feeling in his stomach. One of the vehicles was gone.   Rushing downstairs, Mike was overcome with fear that she had gone and done something stupid, and she did.   They were both gone and the panic set in.

Pacing back and forth, he knew he didn't have much time, as *The Area* was monitored with heat activated motion detectors.   Also there were aircraft in the air to keep an eye on the perimeter to ensure nobody came into Area 51.   All at once, it came to him.   A year earlier, Mike devised an escape route and rally point for the family in case of an emergency.   The escape plans were in three duffle bags in the basement.   Mike rushed down the stairs and two of the bags were gone.   He grabbed the third and raced out to the Explorer.

As he started up the truck, he prayed that he would find them and get them home before somebody flying a Cobra helicopter stumbled upon her and Billy and had to make a split-second decision on what to do.   The pilot might think that they were trespassers, or even terrorists.   He might think they had stolen something from *The Area* and were trying to get it off the base.   He might have orders to shoot. Brian's face popped into his head and he dreaded what was going to happen to his career, or even worse, his family, when this ordeal was all over.

He pulled out his cell phone and made the decision.

It only took the 911 operator one ring to answer, "Is this an emergency?"

"Yes, it is! This is Mike Collins! I live out on West Highway 8 at the Research Estate!"

"Sir, what is the nature of your emergency?"

"My wife has taken my son and I think she is going to try and leave *The Area*! They're in a black Explorer...please make sure nobody hurts them!"

"Sir, do you know where they are going?"

"I think they are heading west, toward Gillman's Ravine! We had maps made with an escape route, if ever needed!"

"Sir, does she have any explosives, or other types of weapons, that we need to be aware of?"

"No, I don't think so! She's just gone crazy or something! Please notify someone...I don't want them to get hurt!"

"Sir, please stay calm. I am typing this into dispatch as we speak which is going directly to the Military Police Headquarters. If there is anyone that has spotted her, I will find out in a moment, and I will inform them that they are not hostiles."

"Oh God, thank you!" He was doing about eighty miles per hour on a dirt road.

After about thirty seconds, which seemed an eternity, "Sir, your wife and son have been intercepted near the area you indicated. The MP's have indicated that they want you to stop your vehicle and one of the other helicopters will be making contact with you within five minutes and will give you a lift."

"What about the Explorer?"

"Sir, that is not a concern at this point. It will be taken care of."

The helicopter ride to wherever they were taking him seemed like a long one. He was so upset, he could feel the heat coming off his face. On one hand he wanted to grab her and scream, "What the hell were you thinking?" but on the other, he knew she had been out of her senses lately with all of the things that had been going on.

She was dealing with the fact that they were bringing a new life into a world that was dying; an ironic beginning of life. Into a world that would be ending in about seven years. He thought *What kind of life would this new child have? Where will we be living? What kind of conditions will we live in? Is this the future of mankind?* Mike felt for her and had no idea what was to come.

They placed Mike into what resembled a holding cell; he hoped he wasn't a prisoner. The facility appeared to be a psych ward, padded walls and all. He didn't hear any other people and Mike wondered if Jessica and Billy were near. He was told to "try and get some sleep," which was impossible. Mike wondered *Will I be fired? Will I suffer the same fate as Sukami? What happened to him?* Mike and Jessica knew too much for the government to just say, "Mike, we're going to have to let you go, have a nice life."

The source of their whole nightmare was slowly getting brighter and brighter; it was morning. Mike knew it would just be a matter of hours before he would be sitting before Brian trying to save his career and maybe all three of their lives.

He was escorted to a room that appeared to be a psychiatrist's office. In the middle of the room sat the doctor's desk. Across from that was a very comfortable-looking couch and off to one side, the classic chair you saw in the office of a shrink. One where you're almost in the fetal position, relaxing, which is exactly what they want.

Nobody was in the room. He was instructed to have a seat on the couch and wait for his family to arrive. Next Billy came in, who wanted nothing but a bear hug from Dad. A long bear hug.

"Are you okay?" Mike pushed Billy back to look him over.

"Yes, Dad. I'm really scared!"

"Son, everything is going to be alright! Are you hurt?"

"No, I'm scared! What's going on? Why was I kept from you and Mom all night?"

"Son, I'm not sure, just relax. I can promise you one thing…everything is going to be alright!"

"Where's Mom?"

"I'm not sure Billy, but I think she's going to be here soon."

No sooner than he could get it out of his mouth, Jessica came in with a doctor and Brian. She ran to Mike and all three of them hugged for a few minutes.

"Do you know how worried I was about you guys?" Mike said in a firm yet caring tone.

"I don't know what I was thinking! I felt like I was going crazy! I thought there was no way out but to run!"

"Honey, I love you." Mike replied, looking deeply into her eyes, holding her face with both hands, "Both of you have nothing to worry about...I will always take care of you!" They hugged again; she began to regain confidence in Mike's leadership as a husband and a father.

With a little clearing of the throat, Brian interrupted the moment.

"Folks, I don't mean to break this up, but we really need to sit down and talk...not only about what happened last night, and why, but about the future of *The Collin's Project*. Things like last night don't just happen. This has been brewing for a while Jessica. You know...we have professionals, on site, who can help with these issues. You guys can't let things build up inside until you can't handle it anymore!"

"But this is classified information...how are we supposed to talk to some shrink?" Mike responded.

"Mike, if you would have expressed a concern to me, I would have reminded you that, in the contract you signed, we specifically put in there that a professional therapist would be available to you and your family, free of charge, and that anything regarding this project was able to be discussed with that person. Of course there is only one professional therapist on site assigned to help your family, and he's fully aware of the situation you and your family is in, and," reaching for the door, "Doctor would you mind taking Billy into the other room for a minute?"

"Not at all, Brian...I was just going to suggest that." The doctor escorted Billy out of the office.

"Mike and Jessica...Dr. Cooney is fully aware of the study Mike is doing and what the findings in the past have been. He has been on-duty with these projects for about thirty years. He knows not only what you are going through Mike, but what you are feeling Jessica. Each scientist, and his family, we have had on this project, has had similar reactions to finding out that the world is going to end...it's natural! Dr. Cooney, and I, were fully aware that we were probably coming to a point where you would need help. However, we assumed your family would show different signs first. We never expected, Jessica, that you would try and leave *The Area* with Billy."

"Look, this wasn't pre-meditated or anything...I just came to a point where I had to do something!" Jessica added.

"Well Jessica, we're going to run some psychological tests in addition to the physical testing you went through this morning."

"What testing this morning?" Mike questioned.

"I have been having these pains in my stomach and they think I may have an ulcer or something."

"Well, like I said, we will need to finish some tests today, and if everything goes well, you can go home to Mike and Billy tomorrow."

"She's going to have to stay here overnight?" Mike questioned.

"I'm afraid so. I'm sorry, but when something like this happens, they have a certain procedure we have to go through to ensure something like this won't happen again."

"Oh, I can assure you that this will never happen again," Jessica interjected, "I'm so sorry!"

"Alright, what we need to do now is…Jessica, go ahead and go out there with Billy so I can have a word with Mike. Dr. Cooney will have a nurse escort you to the room where the tests will take place."

Mike and Jessica gave each other a strong, long hug and a brief kiss. While hugging, Mike whispered, "Honey, just relax, there is nothing to worry about, I will make sure all of us are safe. Just take care of yourself and the baby and we'll see you tomorrow. I love you."

As she left, Mike felt that a real ass chewing was about to come.

"Look Mike, everything is going to be alright…" Brian extended his hand.

"Brian, I'm so sorry!" Mike interrupted, "I should have seen signs of this earlier. I would have never thought she would have gone and done something like this. She has been drinking everyday since she found out, and I should have come to you…but I was hoping she would rebound."

"Look, what's important is that the two of you are okay before we continue on with the project. You won't be able to concentrate on the study until everything is alright at home. What I want you to do is relax in here for a while until we get the initial tests back on Jessica and then I'll have someone take you and Billy home." Brian left.

Mike sat down and relaxed in the office for what seemed to be a couple of hours. The soothing music-playing overhead helped him doze off for a few minutes.

Dr. Cooney walked in, "Mike, we need to talk," the doctor sounded distraught.

"What is it? Is everything okay?" Mike was trying to wake up.

"Look, this won't be easy…Jessica has had a miscarriage."

Tears came to Mike's eyes as he knew that this baby had meant everything to her. It was probably the only thing keeping her going after learning of *Sun Death*.

"Are you sure?"

"Yes…unfortunately. I'm very sorry."

"Where is she?"

"Right now she's in a recovery room. We sedated her…she was extremely upset. The best thing for all of you is for you and Billy to go home until tomorrow. We are going to make sure she gets a lot of rest, and if the two of you do the same, everybody will be in a better frame of mind tomorrow."

As they were riding back to the house, Mike couldn't help but have the morbid thought that maybe this had happened for a reason…that it was a blessing in disguise. Mike thought *Did I really want to bring another child into this world? A world that is going to end.* Mike's eyes slowly filled with tears. He wouldn't cry though, not in front of Billy. Billy had gone through enough already and he wanted him to find out about the baby later. Billy was really looking forward to having a little brother or sister and he would be devastated. Billy needed his father to be strong and Mike would have to muster all of his strength to put on a show.

Later that night, Mike cried himself to sleep.

Chapter 5

Spring Break

It had been almost ten long years since Mike had embarked on *The Collin's Project* and he was anxious to complete it-there was about one month left. He didn't know what he wanted more: the project to be over, or to finally find out what was going to happen with the certain *Chosen* people. He knew what he had to do to get his family chosen, but he couldn't shake the thoughts about the millions of other families that were out there who were just as deserving as his. Each time he started to think of the children, the babies, and people just dying, he got a sick feeling deep inside; he would start to feel numb as though it wasn't really happening. He wanted to wake up next to Jessica and tell her all about the bad dream he just had, but it was reality.

However, lately it had been easy to block out these feelings as Mike was filled with joy that his son was coming home for spring break. Billy was twenty-four years old now, and this year, Mike insisted he come home for spring break. The year before, Billy begged to go to Florida for the break, and after Mike and Jessica talked about it, they decided that he could use a week of just being with his friends away from school. They knew the week would be filled with tons of alcohol, under-age drinking and sex, but that's what college is about. Once they came to grips that that was exactly what they did in those days, and it is just a phase young adults have to go through, it was much easier for them to deal with; and Billy deserved a little hiatus. He had been a straight-A student since he started at Yale, and he was working on his Masters Degree. At his age, Billy was more responsible than both of his parents were in their college days.

During the ride home from work, Mike reminisced about his own college days. He was also a straight-A student, but wasn't as fortunate when it came to staying out of trouble. He was an active member of a fraternity and was more of a party animal than a model student. Mike remembered his initiation to get into his fraternity; he had to do some things that he wouldn't forget for the rest of his life.

The initiation began with the consumption of excessive amounts of alcohol; then the torture began. The fraternity brothers made him get completely naked and then put on women's underwear and a bra. After a few of the guys put an absurd amount of make-up on Mike, they made him run up and down the street for fifteen minutes; then they called the police. Mike couldn't get his mug shot out of his head and he knew it would be there for the rest of his life; those were the days.

But this spring break, Billy would spend it with the family. After Jessica's miscarriage, Mike struck a deal with Brian. Billy was able to leave *The Area* and go to college. The only stipulation was that Mike and Jessica had to take their vacation and go see Billy; he couldn't come back to *The Area*. The only reason Billy was coming back this year was because Mike was at a pivotal part of the project and he couldn't leave. Mike agreed to only take a few days off during Billy's visit, so Brian agreed.

Mike knew that by the time he got home, Billy would be there and he couldn't wait to see him. He couldn't wait to throw a football around and have a cold beer together. Mike had become a very lonely man over the last five years with his son moving off to college. He never really appreciated Billy until he was gone.

Mike and Jessica were much closer after Billy went off to Yale. After losing the baby, and then Billy, it was even more important that Mike spent quality time with Jessica everyday…and he did. They stopped taking each other for granted and appreciated the time they spent together. Doing a study about the end of humanity helped their lives; family and happiness were the most important things in life, so they cherished every minute together. And Mike was going to do just that while Billy was home. He decided to make Friday a half day, and enjoy the long weekend with the family. Boy did he deserve it.

Over the previous five years, since Billy was away, Mike had really whizzed through *The Collin's Project*. There were only two questions left, and Mike had a month to get them finished; he was so close…that's why he couldn't take a vacation…that's why Billy had to come to *The Area*.

Mike's conclusions still found that the white dwarf's collision with the sun was going to transpire in the fall of 2005. The government was hoping the angle of the dwarf would change so that it would miss the sun; Mike's job was to find out. He was also trying to uncover whether or not the government had more time to prepare for the disaster.

Mike found Dr. Sukami's name *Sun Death* ironic. Did it mean the death *of* the sun? Or did it mean the inhabitants of earth's death *by* the sun? Either way, there wasn't a positive ending.

Mike couldn't help but fantasize about how the end of humanity was all going to ensue. With the conclusions Mike and Dr. Sukami had derived, the thermonuclear heat given off from the explosion would decimate the earth and the people inhabiting it. Mike concluded that some people on the opposite side of the globe, from the direction of the heat and radiation, may survive initially, but not for long. Within a few days of *Sun Death*, all human, animal, and plant life would be dead.

If *The Chosen* were to survive, where would they live? The first possibility that Mike came up with was a dome of some kind that would withstand the elements outside, but preserve life inside, but the government couldn't hide it unless it was in some remote location. Another possibility was people living inside the earth itself, like

NORAD, which was built inside a mountain and could withstand a nuclear attack if it ever occurred.

One other possibility that Mike came up with, was some kind of space station that people could live on and maybe even search for another inhabitable planet. Mike was obsessed with finding out and he couldn't stop thinking about it; the suspense was like Christmas Eve, times a million, and there was no opening one present early.

Mike still hadn't found out how *The Chosen* were going to be "taken care of" and it was driving him crazy. He called them *The Chosen* because that's what they seemed to be; chosen. Brian kept giving Mike positive reinforcement that the Collins family had nothing to worry about, but he had to stay focused on the project. Just not for the next three and a half days…that was Billy's time.

As Mike walked into the house, he could hear Billy's voice and he headed in that direction. As he entered the kitchen, there stood Billy…beer in hand.

"Hey, what the hell do you think this is, Florida? Let me see some ID son," Mike said. They hugged.

All three of them had a great time the next day. Grilling-out, swimming and four-wheeling in the desert until they were all exhausted. Mike hadn't felt so complete in years; it felt like a family again. He wanted to go back to the days when life was much easier.

After their baby died, Mike and Jessica went through several years of counseling. At first Mike was opposed to sitting in front of a shrink; he was too macho. Once he tore down his egotistical walls and peered into his emotions, he realized that they had issues that had to be dealt with. Ms. Candle was very helpful with healing the wounds inside both of them, but she was gone now. She had retired from her position with the government to pursue her dream of writing a book on Psychology. A replacement for her never came.

Mike, Jessica, and Billy were all exhausted from the days activities and had an even longer day ahead of them. Mike planned an early morning fishing trip for Billy and him-later they would all swim at the lake. Mike eventually excused himself headed up to retire for the evening.

As Mike woke in the middle of the night, he had a severe case of cottonmouth; he drank way too much with Billy. He discovered that Billy had become quite the drinker and could handle his liquor very well. That was important during college, and was always a good bragging tool with the boys. Heading down to the kitchen to get a bottle of water, he noticed that the light to his office was on. Mike didn't recall leaving it on.

Walking toward the door, the thought crossed Mike's mind, that Billy was in there reading Sukami's journal. But he thought that the chances of that were slim because Billy wasn't a nosy person and it was hidden in his desk drawer. His fear came true as he walked in. There Billy sat, reclined back in the office chair, feet up on Mike's desk, reading the journal.

"What the hell do you think your doing?" Mike yelled.

Startled, Billy pulled his feet down and sat up quickly, closing the journal, "Dad...uh...I was just looking around and..."

"In my desk...what were you looking for?"

"Well, I was just checking out things..."

He walked over to him and grabbed the journal out of his hand, "This is none of your business!"

"Dad, it said in there that a dwarf star is going to..."

Mike put his index finger over his lips to quiet Billy and looked around the room as if he was indicating something to his son. Mike grabbed a piece of paper and wrote, *Don't say another word, the house is bugged, lets go outside* on it.

He grabbed Billy's arm and quickly led him out the front door of the house. They walked quite a ways until Mike was guaranteed that any bugs on the outside of the house wouldn't pick up their conversation.

"What the hell were you thinking? I am working on a top-secret project for the government and you think you can just snoop around in my office?"

"Dad, I'm sorry!"

"You're sorry? You're sorry? Is that supposed to make me feel better? There are only a hand full of people on earth that know what you just read, and I'm supposed to just accept that my twenty-four year old son is one of them...and hope that he keeps his mouth shut?"

"Look Dad, I promise I won't say anything to anybody about this!"

"You're God damn right you won't! Look, I'm really pissed right now! I want you to go to bed and I need some time to think about all of this, so I can think about what we're going to do!"

"Okay…but Dad, I'm sorry."

"Yeah…please do what I said!"

Mike stood outside for about fifteen minutes just shaking his head, figuring that he had screwed up again; he should have hidden the journal in a better place. His main concern was that he hoped no one was listening in on them when Billy mentioned the end of the world in his office. If someone had heard that, they were all in for it. He wasn't sure exactly what would happen, but he was sure that Brian would pay them a visit the next morning if someone had overheard that part of the conversation.

Mike figured the only way he could go back to sleep was to take the edge off, so he headed back to his office and broke out the old bottle of Tequila. He had been going through more of it recently, but that didn't concern him now. He took two shots and headed back up to bed.

The tequila really did the job. Mike had an internal alarm clock that never let him sleep past eight in the morning on his days off, and he hated it. Today was different though, he didn't wake up until after ten. Upon waking up, he laid there for a few minutes wondering if he had just had a bad dream…a nightmare that Billy had read Sukami's journal. He remembered locking the journal in his safe after catching Billy reading it, but Mike knew that he had actually left it in his desk drawer the day before; he had to go check. Walking toward the office, he prayed that the journal was in his desk. If Billy had actually read even part of the journal, it could be devastating to the family and the project.

Mike opened his desk drawer-the journal was gone. He grabbed the dial on the safe, but couldn't remember the combination-his mind was fighting his body. Finally pulling the numbers from deep within his brain, his trembling hand gave the safe what it wanted. The stress of the night before hit him all over again…there laid the journal. He could hear Jessica calling him, her voice getting louder; she was coming. Mike didn't want to talk to anyone right now.

"Hey, honey, I thought I heard you come downstairs…good morning. Isn't it beautiful outside?" she was in too good of a mood.

Mike was trying to choose his words carefully and think before he spoke. Not only because the house was bugged, but because he felt like screaming, but didn't want to alarm Jessica.

"Look honey, I'm really not feeling well. I need you to do me a favor and go out to the Explorer and grab my little black bag that I left out there."

"Oh, I grabbed that yesterday for you."

Mike looked her dead in the eyes and slowly repeated himself in a stern voice, "Honey, I need you to go out and get the bag...I know it is out there!"

She could see in his eyes that she needed to at least go out there and check; if nothing else, but to appease him. It was very rare that Mike got upset with Jessica, so she knew when he did, that she needed to take him seriously. Jessica headed out the front door with Mike close behind. As Mike walked past the kitchen, Billy was standing there drinking orange juice out of the carton and was caught off guard. Billy knew his dad hated when he drank from the carton and he would normally get an ass chewing over it. Mike just kept walking, shaking his head in disbelief; he had bigger problems to deal with.

"Mike, what's going on?" Jessica said, walking toward the shed.

"Just keep walking, go around behind the shed."

"You're scaring me."

"Just shut up and keep walking!"

"What's going on Mike?" as they got behind the shed.

"I found Billy in my office last night! He was reading a journal in my office that was in my desk and he knows about the end of the world."

"Oh my God! This is not happening! How did he...how could you leave your journal where he could find it?"

"It was Dr. Sukami's journal. I found it a long time ago, and have been using it as a reference. It was in my desk and I would never have thought Billy would get into it. What are we going to do? Billy also said it out loud, and with the house being bugged, I don't know if..."

"What do you mean the house is bugged?"

He just realized that the secret that he had kept from her for years had just come out and he knew she was going to be very upset.

57

"Mike, are you saying that there are people listening to us, in our home, every day?"

"Yes, unfortunately."

"How long have you known about this?"

"For a few years."

"And you have been lying to me about it for that long?"

"Look, I really didn't have a choice! Brian had a long talk with me after I told you about *Sun Death* and he instructed me not to tell you about the bugs because you were already devastated with the information I had given you." Mike was starting to get perturbed because the focus of their conversation had totally shifted from its original intent, "Look, Jessica, if you want to argue about this, we can do it later! Right now, we have bigger fish to fry! Billy knows that the world is going to end and if someone heard him in the house, we're screwed!"

"What exactly did he say?"

"I found him in there, and I think I asked him what he was doing and then he hesitated for a second and asked if it was true that a dwarf star was and that's it."

"How loud was he talking?"

"Pretty loud."

"What would they do?"

"I'm not sure exactly, but I don't think they would let him go back to Yale. I'm sure he would be confined to *The Area*. It would be too much of a risk for the government to let him go back out into society. Worst-case scenario, I would be pulled off the project, maybe fired and we would lose our exemption and not be taken care of."

"Yeah, but then we could threaten to tell the truth to everyone," she quickly responded.

"That's true. That's why we would probably be under house arrest or locked up somewhere where we couldn't tell anyone. Remember…Brian said Sukami was taken care of…but he didn't say how. For all we know, they could have killed him!"

"Yeah, we're screwed if they heard him. What do we do now?"

"Wait and see if Brian or someone shows up today. Even if they don't, we won't be in the clear until at least Monday when I get off work. If something hasn't happened by then, I think we're pretty much in the clear."

"Mike, even if everything's fine and they didn't hear him, what are we going to tell Billy? He has to keep his mouth shut or we're all going to be in deep shit!"

"Yeah, I know. I'll take care of it."

They headed back to the house and Mike had to figure out exactly how to convince Billy that he couldn't discuss *Sun Death* with anyone.

"Hey Billy, let's go outside for a few minutes and throw the football around."

"Dad, I was just going to go over some homework that I had for the break and..." Billy knew it was time for a talk.

"Now!" Mike said sternly.

"Yeah, I guess it can wait," Billy saw the intensity in Mike's eyes.

As he was walking outside, Billy yet again realized the implications of what he had done. Not only had he disrespected his father by going through his personal belongings, but he had flirted with the disruption of National Security and his father's career. He wasn't sure what would come out of their conversation, but he knew that it was serious.

"Dad, look I'm really sorry about last night. I promise I'm not going to talk to anybody about it."

"That's what we're going to have a little conversation about, son. I have been working for the government for two decades and have busted my ass for them. At the end of this project, your Mom and I will be retiring, with quite a large sum of money and investments that the government has paid me through the years. When I took on this project, I knew it was extremely important, but I had no idea that it entailed investigating the possible end of civilization on earth, or I probably wouldn't have taken it. Well I probably would have, but...anyways. What I am telling you is that there are only a handful of people that know what you know, and I'm not fucking around when I tell you that it couldn't only be detrimental to my career, but possibly our lives, if it gets out to anyone that you know about *Sun Death*."

"*Sun Death?*"

"Yes, *Sun Death*."

"Dad, I have already said it and I will say it again...I'm not going to tell anyone about this. I'll be honest with you...this has scared the shit out of me! I've been freaked out since last night! This is like a bad dream…or a movie or something! It's really scaring me! You and Mom have nothing to worry about, my lips are sealed."

"I want you to promise me that you won't say a word about this to anyone!"

"I promise, Dad."

They heard a vehicle coming off in the distance. Vehicles could always be heard approaching the house because they lived miles from anyone and the gravel road made it quite obvious when someone was coming. Mike figured it was Brian and it was. They came out from behind the shed and greeted him.

"Hey Brian. What brings you all the way out here on a Sunday?" Mike extended his hand.

"Well, this is probably the only chance I'll get to say hello to Billy. It's been years since I've seen him now that he's away at Yale," Brian extended his hand to Mike's son, "Nice to see you Billy, are you having a nice spring break?"

"Yeah, it's been relaxing."

"You're probably used to partying and staying up all night, huh? Is your Dad a little too boring for you?"

"No, actually this is exactly what I needed."

Brian walked over to Billy's car. Mike and Jessica bought Billy a 1998 Mustang 5.0 a year earlier and Billy kept it in perfect condition. They surprised him for Christmas to reward him for all of his hard work at college. They did give him two stipulations with the gift though: he couldn't get any tickets and his grades couldn't slip. They made it clear that if either happened, the car would be taken away, and they even kept his old car just in case.

"Nice car Billy…what is this, a 99?" Brian slid his hand along the ragtop as he walked alongside her.

"No actually it's a 98, but Billy takes perfect care of her," Mike interjected.

"Yeah, it's a 98, but she runs like new…she's my baby."

Brian knelt down next to the right rear tire. He was down around the rear fender area for a second, with his hand in the wheel well, and said, "You might want to make sure there's plenty of air in these. You don't want to get a flat out here in the middle of nowhere."

"Does the tire look low?" Billy came over to inspect.

"No…I guess not, just looking out for you. Well, I better hit the road, this is the day I get my honeydo list."

"A what list?" Billy had no clue.

"A honeydo list you know, she says, honey do this…honey do that," they all laughed. Then there was an uncomfortable silence. "Well, I gotta go. It was nice seeing you Billy…I'll see you Monday Mike." Brian left.

"That was really weird," Mike pointed out.

"What, Dad?"

"Nothing, I guess," Mike didn't want to alarm Billy; but the timing of the visit was odd.

They loaded up the Explorer for a Sunday trip to the lake. The day would be filled with swimming, fishing, and if Brian wasn't at his cottage, some jet skiing. Mike and Jessica went out to the lake every Sunday; that was their day to relax together. Brian had a cottage on the lake, provided by the government, for him and others to use. Brian and his family went to the cottage about one weekend out of the month, and Mike was hoping that this Sunday wouldn't be one of them. Mike didn't want to see Brian, and he wanted access to all of the water toys.

Sunday night came quickly and the family had a great time at the lake. The three of them were the only people at the cottage and enjoyed every minute of it. Mike wasn't looking forward to heading back to work, but he was leaving early Monday and Tuesday to spend some more time with Billy.

Monday and Tuesday went by and Brian hadn't even stopped by to see Mike at the lab. That was a little odd, but Mike was happy that they obviously hadn't heard Billy mention the dwarf in Mike's office; they were in the clear. It was Wednesday and Billy was leaving that evening. Mike always hated saying goodbye to Billy because they were so close. He knew he wouldn't see him again until summer when Billy would be on break again; and the project would be over. This would be the last time Billy would visit them in *The Area*-that was a good thing.

Whenever Jessica had to say goodbye to Billy, it was a thirty-minute ordeal. She would stall for time, bring up conversations about the irrelevant…anything to just spend a few more minutes with him. That was alright with Mike, he didn't want Billy to leave either.

"You know, this summer we could put that sport kit you been wanting on the Mustang? Also, I was thinking of some things we can do with the engine to really soup it up."

"That would be awesome, Dad!"

"Now, Mike, I think this thing's fast enough! And he hasn't got any tickets…knock on wood!"

"Yeah, you're probably right," Mike said as he winked at Billy.

They were all at a safe distance from the house so Mike wanted to make sure that they were all on the same page. Nobody could find out about *Sun Death*.

"Now, Billy, I know what you're going to say, but we need to talk about this one more time. It is imperative that you don't say anything, to anyone, about what you have found out. I want you to understand…I know I already said this, but I can't stress it enough…this is not only a matter of National Security, but possibly a matter of life and death!"

"Dad, I fully understand the importance of keeping quiet about this. But I would like for you to tell me what's going on this summer. I feel like I was only told part of a story and no ending!"

"You already know too much! All I can tell you is that the three of us are all going to be alright. Now you better hit the road, it's almost dark," Mike added.

"Billy, I still don't understand why you are going to drive three hours and then stay in a motel. Why don't you just sleep here and head out in the morning?" Jessica questioned.

"Mom, I told you. If I stay here, we'll be up late…and then in the morning, you're going to want to make me breakfast…we'll all mess around for a few hours. If I stay in a motel, I'm going to get there, sleep, wake up, and hit the road."

"Okay…just trying to help out."

Mike and Jessica exchanged one last hug with Billy before he left.

As Billy left, Mike couldn't help but pray that God somehow gave his son the courage to keep his mouth shut about all that he had learned during the last week. He had confidence in his son. Billy was a very responsible person and Mike felt that he had made it clear how important it was to keep *Sun Death* a secret.

After a half-hour of driving, Billy felt his discovery burning inside. He didn't intend to keep this secret; it was too colossal. He picked up his cell phone and dialed his best friend, Brett.

"Hey John, it's Billy, is Brett there?"

"Yeah, just a minute."

As he waited, he was sure what he was doing was right. Brett and him had been doing different studies together and were the top students in their science courses. They sat together on the Science and Technology Student Board and were looking for that discovery to really set them apart. Not as students, but as scientists; this was Billy's chance to make a name for himself.

"This is Brett."

"Dude, you're not going to believe what I found out while on break."

"Is it about Area 51?"

"Well, sort of. My Dad has found out that..."

Billy's phone went dead. He had already been Roaming and the LCD on the phone read "Signal Failed." He was just about to tell Brett the fate of humanity and his phone cut off. Billy pulled off to the side of the road and messed with the phone for a few minutes to no avail. He was on the one hour part of the trip where he was out in the middle of nowhere and there were no lights to be seen anywhere. The moon was the only thing that lit up the desert and he found it surreal. He shut off the engine, and just sat there, gazing up into space. He could see thousands of stars and several of them blazing across the sky, then twinkling away into darkness.

There were no people around, no vehicles, no noise-just dead silence. He became a little spooked when he saw headlights in his rear view mirror. They grew larger until they were right behind him; it appeared to be a truck or a SUV and it stopped right behind Billy's Mustang. He thought, *Well, I could be stupid and get out of the car and see who it is, or I can get the hell out of here.* He did the latter of the two...and quickly.

The top to the Mustang was down and as he hit the accelerator, he could hear the sand and gravel hit the front of the truck behind him. Looking at his phone, he saw that the LCD still read "Looking for Service" and he needed to use it...now. The truck was obviously following him, as it mirrored his Mustang's every move. The brights, from the truck, were almost blinding and Billy could hardly stand looking in the mirrors. Billy new he had a fast car and it was time to find out how good of a driver he was. Suddenly his phone rang. He had never been so happy to hear that sound in his life.

"Hello…look, I need help! Who is this?"

"Billy, pull your vehicle over…now! You're in a lot of trouble!"

"Who is this?" Billy ended the call assuming the signal was back, and it was. He quickly dialed 911 while sliding around the dirt road traveling eighty mph; it wasn't an easy task.

"Billy, you can't call anyone on this phone," the voice on the other end said, "We have a direct satellite link to your phone and your vehicle right now. You might as well pull over. Even if you lose us, your car is bugged and we'll find you."

As soon as he said that, Brian kneeling down and reaching into his rear wheel well, played over and over in his head. They knew Billy found out about what his Dad called *Sun Death*; there was hell to pay now.

"Look, I wasn't going to tell anyone anything!"

The truck behind him was right on his bumper and as Billy would veer to one side, it would follow. Speeding up didn't do any good, as the vehicle was at least as fast as his. Suddenly the two vehicles were lit up like a star on stage at Carnegie Hall. A vibrating searchlight, from a helicopter above, was now following both of them and Billy found himself not knowing what to do. Billy had to escape these people or he might die.

They had traveled out of the flat desert and were now in a more hilly area with deep ravines and many curves in the road. Billy felt that he might be able to lose the truck, but the helicopter would be much more difficult, if not impossible, to elude. Even if he did lose them both, his car was bugged and it would only be a matter of minutes until they found him; he had to try. With everything that was going on, Billy had forgot that he had someone on the other end of the phone, which was sandwiched between his hand and the steering wheel.

"Look…do you know who my Dad is? He is going to be really pissed off when he finds out what you guys are doing!"

"What makes you think he is going to find out?" the voice said in a deadly calm manner.

The phone went dead.

The truck was pulling up on his driver's side and Billy could see the silhouettes of at least four men in the vehicle. It was a black Suburban and the widows slowly lowered exposing faces. The two men on the passenger's side reached out the windows with what were obviously guns. As the shots rang out, Billy could tell that they were aiming at the tires. He veered the Mustang hard into the truck, pushing it away to the left side of the road. The driver came back hard at his Mustang and that was all that it took.

Billy's car headed right off the edge of the road into a two hundred foot ravine. As he soared through the air, he felt as though he was flying in slow motion. He thought about the seatbelt he had taken off while sitting in the desert, but he couldn't move to try and fasten it. In the few moments he had before his instantaneous death, his whole life, as short as it was, flashed before his eyes. And Billy's final thought was what was going to happen to his father, who was also his best friend.

As the car hit the bottom of the ravine, it exploded into a fireball shooting one hundred feet into the air. The government vehicle pulled off to the side of the road and all four men got out and quickly surveyed the wreckage. Upon realizing that there was no way Billy could have survived the crash, the driver sent one man out to make sure he hadn't been ejected from the vehicle prior to it hitting. The helicopter also searched for a body and the other three men surveyed the area. They also used night vision goggles to ensure there were no witnesses in the area. They weren't in the restricted area anymore and they knew that it was common for hikers to be out there. There couldn't be any loose ends.

The fire couldn't be seen from a distance; only the walls of the ravine were lit up. As the helicopter landed, a man in a black suit exited the aircraft and headed over to the edge of the ravine; he stared down at the wreckage. It had been fifteen minutes since the explosion, but the flames were still bellowing from the car.

"Just let it burn. The longer it burns, the less identifiable everything will be and the less evidence. I want the wreckage outta here and hidden before sun-up and the body to the morgue in the morning. I'll take care of notifying the family. Good job guys."

Chapter 6

Over the Edge

It had been two weeks since Mike and Jessica had learned Billy had died in the fiery crash in the ravine. Mike found himself out at that edge of the road every afternoon, wondering why this had to happen to his son. The investigators told them that Billy had been traveling at an excessive amount of speed and that he must have lost control of his vehicle and veered off the road. It wasn't like Billy to be driving on a dirt road, in the middle of the night, at what the investigator estimated to be about eighty miles per hour.

He sat at the edge of the ravine daily wondering why some person, some murderer on the loose, who deserved to die, couldn't have driven off the road to his death. Mike wasn't a religious man, and it was times like this that helped reinforce why he had little faith in religion. Although he was a little ignorant towards religion, he would never go so far as to say he didn't believe in God. He felt that if someone said that, there was the possibility that they were destined for misfortune and misery in their life. One instance in Mike's life kept religion in the back of his mind, and left the door open to the possibility of someday worshipping God.

One cold day in December of 1990, his father, Robert, was working under the hood of his Camaro. Somehow the hood of the car collapsed and when he reached out to catch it, his arm snapped. He thought he was in perfect health, though twenty pounds overweight, and even ran in a 5k the month before. The doctors found two holes in the humerus bones of both arms, and within a week, he was diagnosed with cancer.

Three months later, Bob had gone from a borderline genius, to a man who couldn't have a conversation with someone while the television was on. The cancer had spread throughout his body and slowly into his brain and lungs. It slowly ate away at everything precious in his body; every piece of life, until he didn't have any strength left to try and survive. He wasn't a man of words, but a man of actions, and the week before he died was the first time in Bob's whole life that he told Mike that he loved him.

Several days before he died, Bob mentioned that angels were talking to him in his sleep and asking him to go with them, but that he didn't want to go. The day before he died he said that they were there for him again. Bob's parents told him that it was time for him to go with them, and he did. Mike couldn't help but believe that there was "something" out there after that experience and it kept his mind open...at least a little.

Mike wanted so badly to jump off the edge of the ravine and be with his son, but he couldn't leave his wife; leave Jessica alone on the dying planet. Over the last few weeks, Mike lost all motivation to continue his project, even though Brian had been very understanding. Mike was on a paid leave of absence and he was trying to take care of Jessica, as well as himself. He wasn't sure how long Brian would stay off his back, since *The Collin's Project* was at a halt...Mike had to start thinking of going back to work. He kept telling himself that work might be exactly what he needed to move on in life, but he wasn't sure if he wanted to go on. And how would Jessica go on?

Jessica was a complete basket case. After finding out about Billy, she had to go back to the mental hospital that she was in after losing the baby; she was saying all kinds of crazy things about killing herself. The doctor wasn't sure how long it would take her to come out of it, but he told Mike that it would definitely affect her for many years to come. She would be in the hospital "until she shows significant improvement and we are confident that she will not be a harm to herself or others" they told Mike. This left him alone at home since all of the staff was on a two-week vacation.

It was Thursday night, fifteen days after Billy had died when Brian finally stopped over. Every conversation they had, to that point, had been over the phone and there was always an excuse as to why Brian couldn't stop over.

Mike opened the door, "Hey," he said in a low tone.

"Hey Mike, how ya doing?"

"Okay, I guess."

"And Jessica?"

"Not as good as me. I'm not sure how long she's going to be in the psych ward."

"Is she still saying weird things?"

"No, the medicine has taken the edge off...now she's just depressed."

"You seem to be doing better."

"Yeah, I wanted to talk to you. I would like to take next week off and come back the following Monday. That'll give me a little more time to get back into the right frame of mind."

"Whatever you need, Mike."

"There's another thing. I know it's been crazy and all, with Jessica being in the hospital, but we haven't even been able to see the body or even talk about a funeral or anything."

"Mike, I am going to be honest with you...you don't want to see the body. It would only make things worse."

"I need some kind of closure. What if it's not him? What if there's some kind of mistake or something? Maybe he was ejected from the car and is still alive!"

"Mike, the doctor confirmed the dental records...it was Billy in the car."

Mike started to cry, "I just don't know what to do. Jessica is in no frame of mind to have a funeral. We can't even invite relatives to a funeral here. I have to get back on the project. I don't know what to do!"

"Look, just take next week off and relax. Hopefully Jessica will get a little better and then we can talk about a funeral, okay?"

"Yeah."

"Alright, I have to get home. If you need anything, I mean anything at all, call me at home or on the cell, okay?"

"Thanks."

"Alright, take care…I'll talk to you in a few days."

"Okay."

That night Mike decided to hit the Tequila a little harder than usual and just relax and watch television. It was about ten o'clock when the phone rang.

"Hello!"

"Mr. Collins?" it was a young voice.

"Yes, who's this?"

"Hey, how ya doing, this is Brett."

"Brett?" Mike's mind wasn't working as quickly as normal.

"Yeah, Brett. Billy's roommate from Yale."

"Brett! Yeah, sorry, I was half asleep. How are you doing?"

"I'm doing alright. How are you and Billy's Mom doing, though?"

"About as good as can be expected."

"We just found out a few days ago what happened to Billy, and I thought I should call you."

"Well I appreciate that Brett."

"What night did it happen on?" Brett asked in a weird tone.

"It was two Wednesday's ago…why?"

"That's what I thought. I wanted to tell you that I was speaking to him on his cell phone after he left there."

Mike sat up, put the bottle down, and muted the television.

"You were talking to him right after he left here?"

"That's right! I'm scared to talk to you about this, but I'm sure it's nothing. It's just all kinda weird how this all played out…sorta like a movie."

"What do you mean?" Mike asked.

The phone went dead. Mike hung up the phone and then tried to get a dial tone. His heart started to pound, and for a split second, he wondered what was going on. He thanked God for inventing Caller ID and he grabbed his cell phone.

He was shaking as he dialed, "Brett, is that you?"

"Yeah, I tried to call you back and it said that all circuits were busy."

"Look, Brett, I want you to talk fast! Finish what you were saying!"

"Well, Billy called me and said that I wasn't going to believe what he had found out on spring break."

Mike could now feel his heart pounding in his neck, "What did he tell you?"

"I asked if it was about Area 51, and he said something like, sort of or yes...I don't remember. But then he said that you had found out that..." Brett stopped talking.

"That what, Brett? What?"

Mike's cell phone started breaking up.

"That was it! The phone went dead! I tried to call him back, but it said that all circuits were busy, just like now!" Brett was yelling.

Mike could barely hear him now; there was so much static.

"Are you sure that was it?" Mike shouted back.

"Yes! What's going on? Is that your phone or mine?"

"I'm sure it's mine!" Mike responded and the line went dead.

Mike looked at his cell phone and saw the words "Signal Failed." He wasn't sure what to think. He tried his house phone again and there was no dial tone. He didn't know what to do. He knew the house was bugged. Had someone just cut off the connection on both phones? Mike new a little about technology and it would be easy to disconnect the home line, but it would take a few minutes for a satellite to lock in on his cellular signal which would explain why he had a few minutes to talk to Brett.

Even if someone was listening to Mike's conversation with Brett, what would they have gotten out of it? They really didn't discuss anything way out of the ordinary. Billy called Brett, was about to tell him something, and the phone went dead. It wasn't a big deal. At least Mike hoped not.

But what Mike learned was a big deal. He thought, *Did the government tap into Billy's cell phone? Did they try to shut him up? Was it really an accident or was he murdered?*

Mike decided not to focus on what had just happened on the phone. It could have been a coincidence. He would let them make the first move, if there was one. He was suspicious now and was going to use the next week to do some investigating.

The next day Mike headed back out to the scene where Billy headed off the road. He knew that that was the place to start his own investigation and that the longer he waited, the less likely he would find any evidence. He found himself dumfounded that he was even conceiving that the government had anything to do with his son's death. He figured what had happened was a series of coincidences, but he had to make sure.

Mike scaled the path within a couple hundred yards of where Billy headed off the road. He found nothing walking away from the ravine, but upon heading back, he found what was a two-foot long piece of chrome trim; it appeared to be from a vehicle door. He knew Billy had chrome trim custom fit around his wheel wells and doors; Billy thought it was cool. He took the piece of trim, hoping to look at the wreckage later on in the day. The chrome was bent in the middle and had some black paint on it. Mike thought, *If this is Billy's trim from his door, could someone have rammed into him and caused him to head off the road?* Again, he hoped it was coincidental, but he was starting to draw his own conclusion as to what could have happened out in the desert that night.

Mike knew he had a right to see Billy's vehicle, but he never thought it would be so difficult to do so. After three days of calling everyone he could think of, he finally was directed to a facility that had the car-even Brian had given him a hard time. The only thing he could think of was that they were trying to hide something...or stall. If he found the trim missing, there was definitely something fishy going on.

Upon seeing the remains of the Mustang, Mike began to weep. He prayed that Billy was killed on impact, and hadn't been burned alive in the wreckage. The car obviously had burned for quite a long time, as everything that wasn't steel, had melted away. Mike asked for a few minutes alone so there would be nobody around. He knew they would think it was because he was upset, but he wanted to do some snooping.

He looked at the passenger side door and could see the wedge that the chrome trim was in, and the remnants of it melted. As he looked at the driver's side, the wedge was there, but it was completely empty, as though there was no trim in there to melt. Mike had the piece of trim, which he bent in two, down his pant leg and tucked into his sock. Holding the trim up to the door, it was exactly the right size and there was a large dent in the door right where the trim was damaged. Mike's heart started pounding and he felt deep, intense anger. Eyes watering, he quickly put the trim back in his pant leg and decided it was time to go home to regroup his thoughts.

One thing that really bothered Mike, as he sat in his office that night, was that he didn't know for sure that Billy was even dead. They wouldn't let him see the body, for his own good, and he was taking Brian's word, who he didn't even trust. Did the Coroner just assume it was Billy? The answer was so simple. He would call their dentist in California, who had all of their dental records, and find out if anyone had requested a copy of them. Of course, he did have to keep in mind that his home phone was tapped and he was sure now that they had an instant tap to his cell phone.

However, Mike was a step ahead of the government. A year earlier, while on vacation, he purchased six pre-paid cell phones and cards with minutes on them. He paid seventy dollars per phone, plus the cards to activate them. He just stored the phones in case he ever needed them. With his house and cell phones, the government had his number on file and could pull the plug quickly. With the pre-paid phones, he could call them up and activate a phone in minutes, without the government knowing before hand. He knew the batteries would be dead so he opened one up and charged it overnight so he could make the phone call first thing in the morning.

The next day Mike contacted his dentist and found that nobody had requested a copy of any of their family's dental records. But he still wasn't positive that the government had anything to do with Billy's death. If they wanted dental records of Mike's family, without the dentist knowing, they could get them. Mike's next plan was to call the Coroner and try and catch him in a lie. For this one, he would have to use his regular phone. If the Coroner was in on it, he would immediately tell Brian that Mike called and there wouldn't be any record of it.

Mike tried all day to get ahold of the Coroner with no success. After leaving ten messages, he headed out to his office to make personal contact with him. As he stood face to face with the man who pronounced his son dead and supposedly identified him, he felt a real sense of distrust. The man appeared nervous and he was real fidgety.

"John, I'm Mike Collins," Mike extended his hand.

"I'm sorry we had to meet under these circumstances," the Coroner said sympathetically.

"You're a busy man. I have left you about ten messages today."

"That damn secretary! It's hard to find good help nowadays!"

"Actually, I just spoke with her and she said she gave all of the messages to you personally."

"Look, I'm sorry Mike. I'm a very busy man, and I usually call all of my messages at the end of the day," he was getting irritated, "What exactly did you need?"

"Well our dentist, Dr. Tom," knowing it was Dr. Andrews, "contacted me, concerned that maybe you had received the wrong dental records." Mike could tell that John wasn't a good liar and was extremely nervous now, "They think maybe they sent Jessica's by mistake. Can we go check them?"

"No...the dental records are correct. Dr. Tom's office contacted me yesterday, and, as a matter of fact, I actually spoke to Dr. Tom personally, and assured him that we have the accurate documents."

Not only was he an awful liar, but he was extremely stupid to lie and say that he actually spoke with Dr. Tom. Now Mike was going to go home and wait for a visit from Brian, which was sure to come shortly.

Mike went over the evidence he had so far. He thought, *Billy found out about Sun Death and the government may have heard him talk about it in the house. He called his roommate, Brett, to tell him the secret, and Brett's phone went dead. He died in a fiery crash in the middle of the desert, with no witnesses, and supposedly, no other vehicles involved. I have a bent piece of trim, exactly like the piece on Billy's car, which wasn't on the wreckage, and was bent in exactly the same area as the huge dent in his door. I received a call from Brett and as soon as we started talking about the night of the accident, the phone went dead...and then my cell went dead. Now every time I try Brett's number, it says the number is disconnected.*

When I call information, to get Brett's new number, it says there is no listing. I have a Coroner that has lied to me about the dental records and probably Brian who has done the same. The questions that perplexed him were, *"Am I sure?"* and *"What am I going to do about it?"*

He didn't have much time to think about it. The doorbell rang.

"Brian," Mike said as he opened the door. There was another man with him.

"Hey, Mike...this is Special Agent Johnson," they invited themselves in.

"Wow, two of you! What's going on?" Mike was puzzled.

"You tell me! You're the one snooping around!" Brian responded.

"Snooping?" Mike hoped ignorance would work.

"The crash site...the wreckage...and now John's office!"

"Brian, you seem awfully paranoid or something. Do you want to tell me something? Is there something I should know about Billy's death?"

"You act like you know something...if you do, go ahead, let's talk about it," Brian said in a very aggressive tone.

All of the anger from the last few weeks was about to come out. Mike was going to lay it all on the line.

"You're God damn right I know something! Do I look stupid to you?"

"No," Brian replied.

"Well then, I know what the hell happened, and why don't you be a man and tell me?"

"Well Mike, I'm not sure exactly what you're talking about, but..."

"Okay, well if we're going to play stupid, then I'll play," he said furiously, but with sarcasm, "Let's say I went out to the crash scene and found a chrome piece of trim in the dirt road," Brian and the agent looked at each other, "Oh, did we leave a piece of evidence? Oh yeah, I forgot to mention the trim is crunched in the middle. Then let's say I take that down to the wreckage and match it up with Billy's car and it is the perfect size and the door it came off of, which was crunched in also. Now I'm not an investigator, but that would lead me to believe that maybe the car might have been pushed off the edge with another vehicle."

"What are you getting at?" Brian was starting to get upset.

"Then I'm talking with someone on the phone, who was speaking to Billy the night of the accident, and the phone goes dead! Then my cell goes dead! Then you and the Coroner lie about the dental records!"

"Mike, we didn't lie about the records!"

"So you guys got the records from Dr. Tom's office?" Mike asked.

"Yes."

"I can't believe after all of the hard work I have done for you, that you could stand there and lie to my face!" he had got up in Brian's face now. "You asshole! There is no Dr. Tom...it's Dr. Andrews! I spoke with him today, and he hasn't been contacted by anyone regarding Billy's records!"

The agent stepped in and put his arm on Mike's shoulder, "Calm down sir!"

"Get your fucking hands off of me!" Mike pulled his shoulder away.

"You really want to know what happened? Do you really want to know? I don't think you can handle what really happened...that's the problem! You already know what happened...and why! So don't pin this on us!"

"What are you saying?" Mike asked; he was perplexed at what Brian was getting at.

"This isn't our fault! You are the one who was stupid enough to let your son read your journal! That was enough right there, but when he called his friend..."

"Enough for what?"

"We had to take control of the situation! We were on the verge of a breach in National Security and we couldn't let that happen!"

"So you killed him?" tears starting to fill Mike's eyes, as he was about to confirm that his most precious possession on earth was taken away because of *The Collin's Project.*

"We couldn't let that happen at any cost!"

"So you killed him?" Mike was looking for denial or confirmation.

"We didn't kill him…it was an accident!"

"So your people were there?"

"Yes, but our intent was never to kill him! Look Mike, I just found out about Billy the other day! I was told it was an accident! I don't agree with what happened, but at the same time, they couldn't let it get out!"

"Then what would you have done with him to keep him quiet?"

"He would have had to have been sent somewhere or something. Look, we did shut his conversation with his friend off, but then we tried to talk to him and get him to pull off to the side of the road. He thought he could get away or something and there was another vehicle in pursuit, and well, he ended up going off the edge of the ravine."

Mike sat down on his couch, face in hands, and wept for several minutes. He had found a little closure, but he felt like he was on the verge of a nervous breakdown. He wanted so badly to physically hurt Brian and he could barely restrain himself.

"That's it, I quit!" Mike stood up.

"What do you mean?" Brian asked.

"Just what I said," Mike wiped his tears away.

"You can't just quit! We're too close now!"

"Watch me!" Mike started putting his shoes on.

"Mike, I don't think you understand me!" in a bullying tone, "You can't quit, they won't let you!"

"If we are going to use threats, then how about I tell the whole world about *Sun Death* and that the government has known about it since the sixties…how about that?"

The agent stepped in again, "Sir, you better watch what you say, you're on thin ice already."

"You shut the fuck up! I don't even know you!" Mike yelled.

"He's right, Mike…you are on thin ice and…"

"I'm on thin ice? I'm on thin ice? You guys killed my son and you're telling me I'm on thin ice? I'm outta here!" Mike headed for the front door.

Mike took only a couple of steps before the agent grabbed his arm. As he turned toward the agent, Mike balled up his fist and with all of the anger he had built up, he flung his fist around, connecting with the agent's jaw, knocking him unconscious.

Mike saw Brian reaching into his coat and assumed he was going to pull out a gun, so he tackled him. He was right and as they struggled to get control of the gun, Mike head butted Brian, which dazed both of them for a few seconds. Mike grabbed the gun and stood over Brian. He walked around, standing next to his head.

"This is for Billy!" and he kicked Brian in the head, knocking him out instantly.

He checked the agents pulse to make sure he hadn't killed him and he was alright; Mike was in a predicament now. Trying not to panic, he let the ideas flow through his brain. *Should I kill them? Should I tie them up and go get Jessica? How am I going to get Jessica?* Then he quickly devised a plan.

He was going to gag and tie up the agent and put him in the basement. All of the staff was on vacation, so there weren't any witnesses. Next, he would kidnap Brian and use him to get Jessica out of the hospital, and then they would leave. That was as far as he could plan; there wasn't much time.

As he tied up the agent, he couldn't help but feel remorse. He had never done anything like this before, and it felt dreamlike. Mike was a Boy Scout as a kid and knew how to tie a knot that the agent couldn't escape from. Mike first tied up Brian's hands, to ensure he wouldn't try anything while Mike was tying up the agent; Brian had awoken. As he tied up the agent, Mike made Brian stay a very safe distance from the two of them since he had to lay the gun on the floor.

"What are you going to do with me?" Brian asked.

"I should kill you, but I'm not...we're leaving!"

"Look, I told you, I had nothing to do with Billy's death. I just found out the other day...where are you going to take me?"

Mike looked at Brian, and shook his head as he replied, "I'm not stupid. Do you honesty think I am going to tell you where I'm taking you, in front of him, so that they can come find us?" The agent had regained consciousness.

"Mike, you still have time to stop this! I'll tell them to take it easy on you! If this goes any further, I'm not sure that I can help you!"

"Oh, you're going to help me alright! Unless you don't care about your life...you're going to help me!"

Brian just stared at Mike in disbelief. For the first time in their relationship, Mike was in the driver's seat and Brian was along for the ride. Mike was in full control of both of their destinies and Brian had to just wait and see what Mike was going to do next. Before Mike and Brian left to get Jessica, he needed weapons, money and supplies, all of which could be found in the basement. He took all three escape kits from the basement as well as two M-16 rifles, several handguns, some grenades and enough ammunition to supply a small squad of soldiers. He also made sure to grab gas masks and other useful survival items out of Matthew's room. Matthew had shown him exactly where the key was to the munitions locker and had trained Mike on how to use all of the weapons. As he loaded all of the supplies into the Explorer, Brian just stood there, hands bound, in awe that Mike was taking so many supplies and weapons.

"Jesus, Mike! What the hell are we going to do?"

"I'd rather be safe than sorry."

"Come on, do you really think you're going to get away with this? They are going to be looking for me within hours and it will just be a matter of time until they find us!"

"Well, we're going to take our chances! Look, first we are going by the hospital to get Jessica. I swear that if you fuck anything up at the hospital, I will shoot you!"

"You're fucking crazy!" Brian exclaimed.

"Yeah, I am! So I wouldn't advise messing with me right now!" he stared directly into Brian's eyes as he said it and keep staring until Brian looked away.

"How exactly are we going to get her out?"

"Brian, don't act stupid. You have more pull around here than anyone, and all you need to do is tell them what you are going to do. First of all, her doctor probably won't be there when we get there…some nurse or something will be in charge and just tell them what you're doing. Your superiors are in Washington or something…they won't question you."

"You know Mike…not only are you crazy, but you know too much about me."

"I know a lot about you and what you are capable of…and we're going to use that to help us get to Washington."

"Washington? What the hell are we going there for?"

"To meet with The President!"

"What is that going to do? First of all, we won't even make it half way there, and second, if we do meet with him, what are you going to tell him?" Mike didn't respond.

As they headed to the hospital, Mike crossed his fingers that Brian wouldn't make a scene or try to give someone a signal. He would if he was in Brian's shoes, but Mike was more courageous than Brian. He had seen that much of Brian's bullish attitude was for show, and underneath, he was just a cowardly person in charge of many people. He was counting on Brian not proving him wrong at the hospital. Mike felt confident that if they could get out of *The Area*, they could make it to Washington.

They were in and out of the hospital in ten minutes without a hitch. Mike felt that it was too easy and was unsure if Brian had somehow given someone a signal, but he was sure they would find out soon. Mike kept telling Jessica that they were there to take her home, but as they headed the opposite direction, her doubts started to arise.

"Honey, where are we going and why is Brian driving?"

"How are you feeling honey?" Mike responded trying to change the subject momentarily.

"I feel like I'm on drugs or something...my head feels really funny."

"Well, we'll get you some real food if you want. I know that hospital food leaves a lot to be desired, especially after how long you've been there."

"You can say that again. Now where are we going?" she was slurring.

"We're going on a little trip...you have to trust me on this. Try and get some rest and we'll talk about it when you wake up. I'll tell you everything, but I want you to have a clear mind when I tell you," Mike explained.

"What the hell is going on?" she sat up.

"Please, please honey...you have to trust me on this!"

She was exhausted from being in the hospital for several weeks and it had taken a toll on her...not only psychologically, but physically as well. She had spent the last few weeks trying to convince a psychiatrist that she wasn't crazy and that she wasn't a threat to herself or others.

She was still in a state of shock that Billy had died, but had passed the initial feeling of wanting to end her own life. She knew that even though she might have said things about hurting herself, she didn't have enough courage to act on it. However, she understood that when a psychiatrist hears someone say something suicidal or homicidal, they have to respond immediately; that's their job.

"Here, take this," Mike handed her a pill and a soda.

"What's this?" she looked suspicious.

"It'll help you rest for a while. Trust me…I'll explain everything when you wake up."

She stared at Mike, wondering whether his intentions were genuine, but she didn't have the energy to resist. She popped it in her mouth, took a drink, and laid back in her seat. She couldn't hold on. She dozed off to sleep.

Chapter 7

The Trip

A simple nod to the guards at the gate, from Brian, was all that it took for them to get through. They had made it safely out of *The Area* and Mike felt that it was downhill from there. As they were driving through the blackened desert night, Mike got online to plan a route to Washington; he reflected how great technology was-here he was, running from the law, and he could get online with his laptop and plan a journey across the country.

He figured that once the government was on their trail, they would try and analyze what route they would travel. The computer told him to take a straight shot from Nevada to Washington, D.C., which totaled 2,486 miles; that would be too obvious. That trip would take approximately forty-three hours to travel, but Mike pondered as to which route the government was more likely to watch. He could take the obvious route, which surely they wouldn't think he would do, or he could take a more northern or southern route.

Mike decided that it would be smarter to take a longer route to the south. The trip would total almost three thousand miles and fifty-four hours of driving, but Mike thought the authorities were less likely to saturate that route. The trip would entail four stops before getting to the nation's capital: Phoenix, then Amarillo, Little Rock, and Raleigh, before the final leg to Washington.

It would be much faster for the three of them to fly to Washington, but nearly impossible. Every airport in the continental U.S. would be on the lookout for them once the word got out. Even the security at smaller airports would be hard to get through. Their names would be flagged if they even tried to travel by air. Traveling on the road had it's own risks, but Mike thought their chance for success was much higher.

Driving only at night, Mike planned to stay in small hotels on the outskirts of each of those cities, as there would be less chance of being seen. He wasn't sure how much of a head start they would have on their followers, but he had planned on about one day. Mike played it over and over in his head how they would discover that he had kidnapped Brian.

Brian's wife would be the first to become suspicious when he didn't come home from work that night. Also, if the agent in his basement had a significant other, they would be concerned. They would contact the Military Police who would retrace their last steps and it would lead them to Mike's house. They would find the agent in the basement who would inform them of what had happened and all exits from *The Area* would be on High Alert to ensure they couldn't escape. The guard at the Eastern gate would then notify the MP's that he had seen the three of them exit at that gate and the search would be on. Mike was counting on at least a twelve hour, and hopefully a twenty-four hour head start.

"How far do you think we are going to get before they find us, Mike?" Brian asked.

"I'm hoping all the way to D.C.!"

"I still don't understand why you want to go there. What are you going to tell The President?"

"I have something that I discovered a couple of months ago about the project that is vital."

"Like what?"

"I'm not going to tell you. I haven't told anyone about this, not even Jessica! The only person I'm going to tell is The President himself, and only after he lets me off this project and promises that I won't be arrested for all of this."

"Well then, you better hope nobody gets hurt."

"You just drive and do what I say, when I say it, and nobody will get hurt!"

"Look Mike, I'm willing to help you, but first of all, if we are going to make it to D.C., we're going to have to work together and the first thing we are going to have to do is get rid of this truck."

"Why would you help me?"

"Because I agree that you should be let off the project. You have put in a lot of hard work for the government and it's set in stone that *Sun Death* is going to happen and with the last few weeks…"

"Then why the visit and the threats?"

"Mike, you have to keep in mind that I take orders from people very high up and I have to do what I'm told. There's no questioning those people."

"Who are they?"

"You really want to know? They are the Heads of the CIA, FBI, Homeland Security, The Secretary of Defense and The President himself. I report directly to those people. Now could you imagine me questioning them?"

"Not really."

"Exactly."

"What are you two talking about and where the hell are we going?" they heard from the back seat.

"Hey honey, how was your nap?" Mike was trying to diffuse her anger.

"My nap was fine! Now start explaining what's going on!" Jessica was pissed.

"Yeah, Mike…tell her how the two of you are fugitives."

"Fugitives?" she exclaimed.

"Just relax, honey! Look, Billy didn't just crash…he was forced off the road!"

"What…by who? What the hell are you talking about?"

"After he left the house, he tried to call Brett and tell them what he had read in my journal."

"Oh my God, how could he do that? How stupid!" she started balling. Then she turned her anger to Mike, "Why couldn't you have locked that God damn thing up?"

Mike climbed into the back seat to console her. She hugged him with one hand and weakly pounded on his shoulder with the other, "Why did he have to read it? This isn't worth it anymore. I just want us to go away."

"That's what I'm working on," then Mike looked up at the highway just in time, "Brian, take that exit, toward Phoenix."

"I was beginning to wonder if we were heading to Mexico," Brian had an uncanny demeanor. He had been kidnapped, but was acting sarcastic, almost playful; this perplexed Mike.

"So where are we going and what are we doing?" Jessica demanded.

"Well, don't freak out, but I've kidnapped Brian and we're heading to Washington."

"What? Kidnapped! You mean the cops are going to be looking for us?" she asked in disbelief.

"You're going to wish it was the cops! It's going to be more like the whole government," Brian looked at Jessica through the rear view mirror, then smiled. Brian was acting as though he wasn't worried about being kidnapped; almost as if he was relieved *The Collin's Project* was ending this way.

"Shut up!" Mike demanded of Brian, then he looked to Jessica, "Everything's going to be alright, I have a plan."

"A plan to escape from the government. Remember when I wanted to leave *The Area* and you told me there was no way, they would find us? What about that?" she reminded him.

"But we only have to make it for five days. We're going to drive at night and make four stops before getting to D.C. There will be fewer people looking for us at night…don't worry, we'll make it," Mike really needed her approval for things to go smoothly.

"Why don't we just rotate and drive straight through," Jessica thought she had a great idea.

"I already have it planned. One person will be driving. The person in the passenger seat is going to be the lookout. And the person in the back seat is the navigator. This way the driver can focus on driving only...they'll be less chance of breaking any laws."

"Mike, I'm not trying to be pessimistic, but don't you think they have thought of all of this already? Driving at night? Taking a less obvious route?" Brian responded.

"Look, would you please shut up? You're starting to really piss me off!" Mike quickly responded.

"I'm just trying to help. You know I can really help if you give me the chance."

"Or you could really screw us and get us caught. I don't trust you yet...you're going to have to prove yourself first!"

"How do you want me to prove myself to you?"

"Get us to Washington!" Mike exclaimed and the car was dead quiet.

Mike knew that Brian could either be a huge asset to them getting to Washington or a liability and was counting on the first. Brian had connections all over the world and could see to it, if he wanted, that they could make the trip safely, without getting caught. The only problem was figuring out how to motivate him. His initial motivation for Brian was to threaten him, but he wasn't sure how convincing that would be. Another alternative Mike thought of was to get Brian on his side and try and work together as a team, but they would have to trust each other. Mike knew that even if he did get to a comfortable level of trust with Brian, he would still have to be careful. Mike and Jessica's lives were on the line.

Mike gazed out into the stars and wondered how he got into such a huge mess and what the future held for them. He still didn't even know what "taken care of" meant to him and Jessica. Did it mean that the government had a plan for *The Chosen* to escape this tragedy or did it just mean that they wouldn't suffer; they wouldn't burn alive, they would die quickly? The only thing that he was sure of was that they needed to get to Washington and talk to The President; Mike wasn't going to let anything stop them.

The first leg of their trip took them to Phoenix, Arizona. The plan was to lay low and not attract any attention, so they could rest until evening when they would travel again. But the first order of business was to get a new vehicle. With all of the authorities looking for them, they couldn't take a chance of the Explorer being seen at a hotel. Mike had a friend that lived in Scottsdale, and he was counting on his help.

His name was Scott Peters and they had been buddies since High School. Over the last ten years they had only been communicating over the Internet, but Scott owed Mike a huge favor. About eight years earlier, Scott got into trouble with the IRS and was looking at doing some time in prison. He owed over five hundred thousand dollars in back taxes and he insisted it was an honest mistake. After fighting it for four years, the IRS wouldn't even talk to him, or his lawyer, about just letting him pay back the money plus any penalties.

One day Mike and Scott were instant messaging each other on the Internet and Scott explained to Mike what was going on and Mike decided to see if he could help him. Mike called a friend, who called a friend, who called a friend, who called the IRS lawyer and the next thing he knew, Scott was given the option of just paying back the money and an even lighter penalty than he had originally thought. Scott vowed on his parent's graves that if there was anything that he could ever do to repay Mike, all he had to do was just ask; Mike was about to do just that.

Mike pulled out his laptop, got online, and with only a few clicks, got directions to Scott's house. It was 4 a.m. when Mike knocked on Scott's door. After a few minutes, he started to fear that Scott wasn't home or might be on vacation, but then he heard his voice.

"Who is it?"

"It's Mike," he said, knowing Scott would be in awe.

"Who?" the voice inside the house asked.

"Mike Collins from the IRS," he said sarcastically. The door opened.

"What the hell are you doing here, and at 4 a.m.?" reaching out for a friendly hug.

"Can we talk inside?" Mike said in a serious tone.

"By all means," reaching his hand out, "this must be your lovely wife, Jessica?"

"Oh, I'm sorry. Yes, this is Jessica and this is my boss, Brian," Mike responded.

"Pleasure to meet both of you, come on in."

Walking into his home, Mike could see that the tax fraud penalties hadn't hurt Scott financially at all. His home was decorated very eloquently in a Southwest style and was very clean and neat. Looking around, Mike could see statues and artifacts that probably were more valuable than Mike's vehicle. It was apparent that even with his business venture turning sour, he was still a millionaire.

"Is there something wrong?" Scott asked as if he was scared to hear the answer.

"Well, remember when you said you owed me a huge favor?"

"Yeah."

"Well, I really need one."

"Anything, just name it," Scott answered without hesitation.

"Well Scott, I really can't go into much detail...you know I work on top-secret projects for the government, but I need to swap our vehicle for one of yours for a while."

"What's wrong?"

"Like I said, I really can't go into much detail. You're going to have to trust me when I say, it is a matter of National Security that I get to Washington, D.C. and we won't make it if we are driving our truck!"

"Is someone chasing you?"

"Well," pausing for a moment, "Yes."

"Are you in trouble with the law?"

"Well sort of, but not really. If we can make it to Washington, everything will be alright. That's why I really need your help."

"Mike, I told you when you got me out of that jam with the IRS, that I would do anything, anything at all for you, and I meant it."

"You don't know how much I appreciate this," reaching to shake his friends hand.

"Well, I have the Jag and an Escalade. The Jag is red and a convertible so that may draw some attention, plus there isn't much room. You may want to take the truck. It's fully loaded, tinted windows, but not too much so the police would pull you over. Wait...we could fly. I have a Piper PA-28 at the airport."

"The Phoenix airport is too big. Surely they will be looking for us at every major airport in the country," Mike responded.

"No, the Scottsdale airport," Scott responded.

"I didn't know there was an airport in Scottsdale," Mike was curious.

"Maybe not for long. These fuckers buy a house right next to the airport, then they complain about the noise. They'll probably close it someday. It's fucking crazy! This country's amazing," Scott was getting off on a tangent.

"I don't know...what do you guys think?" Mike looked to Jessica, then to Brian.

"Well, it's worth a try...I guess," Brian responded looking to Jessica who nodded.

"Okay, lets do it. When can we leave?" Mike looked to Scott.

"Today."

"How about tonight...we're all exhausted. We need some rest," Mike responded.

"Hey man, Mi casa es Su Casa! Make yourselves at home. You guys hungry?" walking toward his kitchen, beckoning them, "Come on, I'll whip up some juevos rancheros for breakfast. Or would that be dinner for you guys," Scott laughed.

They enjoyed a hearty breakfast and retired to one of the guest rooms. Scott mentioned to Mike that he was working at home all day, so Mike asked him to keep an eye out and make sure that Brian didn't sneak out. Mike could see the uncertainty in Scott's eyes hoping that he wasn't getting involved in something that would turn around and bite him in the ass, but he owed his freedom to Mike so he didn't even question him.

They awoke to the alarm clock and it was seven o'clock in the evening. They had just enough time to shower and get ready for the next leg of their trip.

"Alright, Brian, it's your turn to shower. And after that, I'm going to need you to stay in the bathroom while I take mine," Mike ordered.

"Why don't we just take one together?" Brian responded sarcastically.

"Ha, Ha, real funny. Look, I would really like to trust you, but right now I have to cover my ass."

"Yeah, please. I'd rather not see it while we're in there."

Mike was feeling as if Brian was more relaxed, but wasn't sure if he was playing him and then going to try and make a move; he had to be cautious. He would need Brian to do something really big to gain Mike's trust. He knew the rest of the trip wouldn't be as easy as this leg and figured Brian would have his chance to help the group very soon.

They all jumped in the Escalade and headed to the airport. The SUV smelled brand new. It was loaded; there couldn't possibly have been a feature that the vehicle didn't have. It was black, with a brown leather interior; the rims shined, they were chrome. Mike insisted on driving; he knew he could get them out of a jam if necessary.

"Turn right, onto the 101-North, then we're going to get off on Frank Lloyd Wright and go left. Then we'll make another left and we're there," Scott instructed.

"I've never seen such extravagant landscaping on a freeway. They have purple lizards on the walls...look Mike," Jessica pointed out the window.

"Yeah, that's where the tax money goes. But you know, Scottsdale is the most livable city in the country, they say," Scott was being sarcastic.

"Whatever," Mike responded.

As they pulled into the parking lot, there were four police cars outside the main entrance; Scott looked nervous.

"That's strange," Scott pointed out.

"What?" Jessica was inquisitive.

"Yeah, what?" Mike added.

"There's normally just one cop out here...what do you want to do, Mike?"

"Fuck it," Mike was upset. They were wasting valuable time, "lets go back to your house, we need to get on the road."

"Alright. Sorry man, I had no idea," Scott responded.

"It's not your fault," Mike said.

As they pulled into Scott's driveway, Mike was concerned about the trip to come. He was doubting their ability to make it all the way to Washington on the road; but they had no choice, they had to make it.

The first leg of the trip had taken twelve hours and entailed four hundred and thirty five miles of driving. Getting to Amarillo, Texas, would take the same amount of time, but they would cover three hundred and seventeen more miles. Mike had printed out each leg of the journey on a portable printer that was connected to his laptop. To ensure that the government wouldn't find their location while online, Mike had to pull off some ingenious computer hacking.

With the use of his new cell phones, he got online through a small online server out of the Philippines. He had to have all of his information encrypted on the computer so that it would make it even more difficult if they did tap into what he was looking at. Mike would never spend more than a couple minutes online to ensure that it would be virtually impossible for anyone to track where they were.

"Where are we heading now?" Brian asked.

"We're on to Amarillo, Texas," Mike responded.

"And after that?"

"Why?" Mike said in an untrusting tone.

"Look, this is going to be a long trip and I just want to know," then pausing a few seconds, "you really don't trust me, do you?"

"Look, I would love to trust you, but we have to make it to Washington!" Mike stated passionately.

"I don't understand what is so important that you have to go through all of this to talk to The President."

Mike sensed that Brain was prodding for what he had discovered about *Sun Death.*

"Brian, if you want to earn my trust, why don't you give me some information…like what has been going on in *The Area* and for how long?"

"You don't want to know."

"Yes, I really do."

Brian paused for a few moments and let out a huge breath of air before responding.

"Mike, look what I'm about to share with you could cost me my job and possibly my family's chances of getting out of this God forsaken mess…"

It all started on July 2, 1947 in Roswell, New Mexico. Two people spotted an object in the sky that was fifteen to twenty feet in diameter, about fifteen hundred feet up in the air, and was traveling about five hundred miles per hour. The story was reported in the Roswell Daily Record, but the real story was never published.

The object in the sky was a UFO that was shot down by the United States Air Force. The crash site, when discovered, included the burning wreckage and three extra-terrestrials, one of which was still alive. Quickly the government took control of the area and took all civilian witnesses away for interrogation; they were never seen again. The wreckage was transported to Area 51 along with the two dead aliens and the one that was still alive.

Two weeks later the alien died along with the government's hopes of communicating with it. The scientists spent years sifting through what was left from the wreckage and found vast amounts of information that helped with future technology, but that information wouldn't be the most important that they had uncovered. Inside the UFO they found what appeared to be a book, with different hieroglyphics in it; it would take a group of four scientists over sixteen years to decipher their meaning.

After cracking the code to the book, it appeared that it was a journal, that included why the aliens had come to earth and what they were supposed to do on their mission. Apparently, the three aliens were sent from their leader to warn the people on earth of their findings about a planet heading toward the sun at a very high rate of speed. It was a white dwarf star-it appeared that it would collide with the sun sometime in the fall of 2005. They were also given instructions to share technology with the humans to speed up earth's space travel capabilities with the hope that many, if not all, people could escape before what the book called *Sun Death*.

The government's first order of business was to confirm the information they had received before any plan of action would get underway. They put their top scientist on the project in 1963 and after seven years, he had drawn the same conclusion. Then in the 1970's, they put another top scientist on the project and he too confirmed *Sun Death*. Still wanting confirmation, they hired Dr. Sukami in the early 1980's to do the same study, without any hint of the previous findings, and he also came to the same conclusion.

"And that's when you guys killed his daughter?" Mike interjected.

"Mike, I'll be honest with you...from what I've been told, that never happened. I know that's what he thought, but I don't think that's reality! How did you get that information anyways. You found his journal, didn't you?" Brian questioned.

"Yes, I did."

"Do you have it with you?"

"Maybe."

"Get back to the story, I want to know everything," Jessica interrupted.

"Okay, I'll get back to it, but only if Mike promises to show me the journal."

"Why should I?" Mike was trying to be an ass.

"Well, you do want me to tell you everything, right? I even have information about the evacuation plans and information on the space station…some of it you won't believe and it's all right here in my laptop," tapping it like he was bartering, "Trust me, all of this gets much more interesting."

"Space station?" Mike exclaimed.

"Yeah! Where do you think we are going to escape to?"

"Alright, I'll show it to you…but only after you finish," Mike conceded. He had to know everything.

"Deal," Brian confirmed.

As Brian continued, Mike found out that he was the fourth scientist hired to confirm the results and that a major evacuation plan was already underway to get several hundred of *The Chosen* people off the planet to live safely on a space station. Mike would be the last scientist hired as his study would finish just a few months short of *Sun Death* and there would be no need for any further research. They were paying Mike to see if anything had changed with the speed and trajectory of the dwarf star that would give the government more time.

"Brian, before you explain the evacuation plan, we need to stop at the next truck stop. I need to make a phone call."

"Who do you need to call, honey?" Jessica responded with curiosity.

"The President!"

"What for? You know they can trace that?" Brian pointed out.

"Do I look stupid enough to let that happen?"

"Hey, whatever you want to do, it's your show Mike," Brian shook his head in disbelief.

As he saw the billboard for the next truck stop just a few miles away, he anticipated what he would say to The President. He wanted to let him know that he had vital information regarding the study to bait him into meeting with him, but he had to be cautious. He really did have some vital information about *Sun Death*, but he couldn't tell anyone yet; even Jessica didn't know what he had uncovered. Just as they reached the truck stop, rain started pelting the truck and it wasn't just a drizzle; it was pouring.

Mike entered the phone booth, which was one of the older freestanding ones where he had to pull the door shut. The rain was pelting the roof of the booth and he quickly thought that it may help give away their location, but then concluded that it could be raining at hundreds of places across the U.S. at the same time. Brian had given him a direct line to The President and after dialing it with a trembling index finger, it rang twice.

"This is Mr. Rotin, how may I help you," the voice answered.

"Yes, can I speak to The President, please?" something Mike never dreamed he would actually be asking.

"May I ask who's calling?"

"Mike Collins," he responded, hoping his name would ring a bell with the voice on the other end.

"Oh! One moment, please," Mr. Rotin responded as if he had just been having a conversation about Mike.

He held on the line for what seemed to be an eternity, constantly looking at his wristwatch to make sure he wasn't on the line too long to be traced. After about thirty seconds, Mike hung up. He stood there for a few minutes and pondered on what to do.

"Hey, bud, you gonna use that phone or just stand there…it's pouring out here?" a man yelled as he banged on the door.

"Sorry, I'll just be a few minutes longer," Mike angrily responded knowing he couldn't stall any longer, so he dialed again.

"This is Mr. Rotin, how may I help you?" with the exact same monotone voice.

"Yes, this is Mike Collins, I just called," in an aggressive tone, "I need to talk to The President and don't put me on hold for long. This is an emergency!"

"One moment please," and he was on hold again.

No more than five seconds later, "Mike, this is The President."

"Yes, sir. This is Mike Collins."

"You know, you're in a lot of trouble! You better turn yourself in."

"Look, I can't talk long. I know you guys are going to trace this. It is vital that I meet with you regarding *Sun Death*."

"Let's not mention this on this line, there are people listening."

"Well then you need to meet with me or there are going to be two hundred and fifty million people listening to me!"

"Now, you're not in any position to be threatening anyone right now!"

"Mr. President, you're wrong! I *am* in a position to threaten! Look, it doesn't need to come to this…I have vital information that I don't think you are aware of with the study I have been working on. I don't think accurate information has been given to you regarding the study. Look, I'll call you back tomorrow, I gotta go," and Mike hung up.

As quickly as he pulled open the door to the phone booth, the man waiting grabbed Mike's jacket, pulled him out gently, stepped into the booth and nicely said, "It's about time, asshole." He slammed the door in Mike's face.

The rain started turning to hail and Mike ran for the cover of the building. He was leaning in the corner and the area he was in was dark as night. Brian and Jessica were waiting in the truck for him, but could tell that Mike was waiting for a quick break in the weather before making a run for it.

Suddenly Mike heard tires squealing and looked to his left only to see a black Expedition, moving at a high rate of speed, racing through the parking lot, then turning sharply around some cars. It sped past Mike and slammed on the breaks right in front of the phone booth. Two men jumped out of the truck, ran to about ten feet from the man in the booth and opened fire with automatic machine guns. As the men shot, the inside of the shattered glass was being coated with blood. It was surreal, something out of a movie. But there were no gunshots, the bullets exited the guns with an eerie silence; these were professionals and they were using silencers. Even the sound of the shattering glass couldn't be heard above the pelting rain. They emptied their clip and reloaded, only to empty it again. The men seemed as though they had no care in the world of law enforcement with all of the time they were taking and bullets they were expending on the body. As their clips emptied the second time, they jumped back into the SUV and it sped off into the night.

Mike knew there was no coincidence that this had just happened and he knew he was the target of the gunmen. He hoped The President hadn't ordered the strike, but he wasn't sure. He figured it was probably someone else, possibly from the CIA or someone atop one of the hidden departments that the public never hears about. He knew their only chance was to reach The President himself. And he knew now, more than ever, it was a matter of life and death.

Chapter 8

The Plan

As they continued on their journey to Amarillo, Mike was numbed by the recent incident. He felt as though his mind was in a state of shock. Jessica had been going on and on hysterically-screaming, crying, sobbing. After twenty minutes, something had to be done to shut her up. Brian pulled the vehicle to the side of the road and convinced her to take some pain medicine to calm her down. She was out cold.

They made it to a hotel just past Amarillo; that would be their resting point. As Mike checked in, he was nervous of being recognized. He tried not to make eye contact with the person at the desk, but was also self-conscious of being too obvious. They made it to their room and Jessica and Brian fell quickly to sleep. Mike wasn't as lucky, as his anxiety had taken over his mind. Another sleepless night.

Mike was jealous of them being able to rest. It had been almost a week since he had actually slept soundly for more than an hour or so. It was catching up to him. His body needed some rest and it needed it soon, but Mike couldn't see it happening in the foreseeable future.

Their trip was far from being over. After they reached Amarillo, they would have a ten hour drive to Little Rock, then fifteen hours to Raleigh, and finally a short five hour drive to D.C. And when they would arrive in the nation's capital, that's when the real work would begin. Mike couldn't rest much in the hotel rooms, and if he did, it wouldn't really be rest. His paranoia of Brian escaping would halt any real attempt of his mind falling into a deep sleep. His rest would have to come while Brian was driving; he hated sleeping in cars.

Evening came and Mike hadn't spoken a word to Brian since the incident at the truck stop. About an hour into their driving, Brian spoke.

"You know I warned you about them tracing that call?"

"You know Brian…I was just thinking, *Man, I can't believe Brian hasn't said, I told you so yet and been a know-it-all about the shooting. Maybe he's starting to change,* but you know, you just proved me wrong…again!"

"I'm just saying, if you want to make it to see The President, take some of my advice. I know these guys that are tracking us. For God sake, I am those guys! I spent twelve years at The Agency!"

One of the things that Mike really hated about Brian was that he always had to either be right or win at everything he did. Even when he was wrong about something, or lost, there was always an excuse as to why. He was the most competitive person Mike had ever met, but it had also made Brian very successful.

Brian was never the most popular person at work, but he worked hard to get where he was and he demanded respect. And if you reported to him, he was always going to win or be right.

"I know. It was a bad call! And that poor bastard that yanked me out of the phone booth…"

"Forget about him! He died quickly compared to what would have happened to him in a few months."

Mike refocused, "Yes, we need to see The President. I need to talk to him about the future of mankind."

"You have made a couple of comments like that now," Brian stopped the car, "You make it sound like you've found something that the other scientists didn't. Did you?"

"Yes, I did. But the only person on this planet that I will tell is The President. Now, we need to get back to your story. I want to know about the evacuation plan. Like, when did it start, how are they pulling it off without the whole world knowing, etc.?" and Brian continued.

The plan was to evacuate about four hundred people, not including the crew, to a space station. It wasn't the International Space Station, but one that no one knew about back on earth. It was much larger than the ISS and its purpose was to be a vessel that could sustain life as well as search for a new planet. *The Station*, as Brian called it, was ready for life in the year 2000. The evacuations would start on January 2, 2005, though it wouldn't be fully operational until sometime during the spring of 2006.

Most of what people on earth thought they knew about all missions to outer space weren't true. All of NASA's missions that the world saw on television were staged. Brian explained that a crew would be sent up to *The Station* to work on certain things, or deliver certain people, but what people watched on television was staged by what Brian described as the government's version of Hollywood. The actors were performing all of the duties of a real mission to space, but it all took place on earth. The real astronauts were going back and forth to *The Station* delivering people, and supplies, vital to the success of the evacuation. The government was so good at staging the missions, that ninety-nine percent of NASA didn't even know about it; the other one percent were part of *The Chosen* and were in on it from the beginning. Brian also confessed that this was exactly how they faked the mission to the moon.

"So you're telling me that we never walked on the moon?" Mike was a little upset.

"Yup, it was all staged," Brian paused for a moment, and then he pulled the car to the side of the road again, "Look Mike...things like this have been going on for a long time. Things aren't always what they seem. The United States Government is the most powerful and influential group of people on the planet! They know how to snowball all of humanity into believing whatever they want. This goes much, much deeper than even I know! Just wait until I get into the cloning that they are doing up there. Now let me get back to how the missions started, I want to start at the beginning."

He explained that there would be a minimum of one mission per week, from the outset, until all of *The Chosen*, and all supplies, were on *The Station*. The first group of people to be taken to *The Station* was all of the crew, which consisted of about fifty people. Then slowly as earth moved closer to *Sun Death*, more and more of *The Chosen* would be evacuated to *The Station*. The government decided to evacuate all of the lowest profile people first and move up the ladder until eventually The President himself would go up.

Brian went on to explain that The President would address the world once he was safely on *The Station*. The plan was to address the world from a stage that would look exactly like the Oval Office so people on earth would believe that he was still on the planet. The address to the world would take place just twenty-four hours before *Sun Death*. The goal was to hide the fact that The President had abandoned the people on earth and trick them into thinking that the government had just learned about the tragedy to come. He would tell the people on earth that they could survive if they would follow the government's plan; that they could survive without the sun. But, he had to do this without hinting that half of the world would be burned alive during the initial pelting of the earth by the suns heat and radiation.

It had been calculated that the initial heat and radiation would hit the Eastern Hemisphere of earth which would lessen the initial deaths of people in North and South America. It would stop them from being burned alive, but many would still die due to the increased temperature across the globe and the weather conditions that would follow. Also the atmosphere would eventually deteriorate. But nobody on earth would know that terrifying fact-only *The Chosen* knew. The President would hope that the American public was ignorant and didn't understand that earth couldn't survive without the sun.

"You mean, everyone would die without the sun?" Jessica questioned.

"Of course, honey. Look…" Mike interrupted Brian. The sun was fascinating to Mike, and he had plenty of information to share with Jessica and Brian. Too much.

Mike explained that the sun gives people on earth heat, light, their food, and the air they breathe. It powers the atmosphere to give them wind and rain. It also heats the air, land, and oceans. The sun evaporates water from lakes and oceans and when the water vapor cools, it drops as rain or snow. This moisture is needed for drinking water and for plants and animals to grow.

"So you're saying it wouldn't rain without the sun?" Jessica was skeptical.

"Honey, there wouldn't even be any clouds. Now check this out," Brian and Jessica looked at each other like they wanted him to stop and Mike caught them, "come on, you guys got me started. Look, this is really interesting…you may learn something."

Mike went on to explain. Some plants use the sun's rays to turn carbon dioxide and water into carbohydrates. During that process, they also release oxygen that people and animals use to breathe. Then humans and animals breathe the oxygen and release carbon dioxide and the whole process starts over.

"So we couldn't breath either," Jessica asked in disbelief.

"Honey, I've told you all of this before! Don't you remember? If plant life dies, eventually we die. Why do you think they are so worried about the rain forest in South America?" She shrugged her shoulders. Mike was a little disappointed that she didn't know much about his beloved planet.

"How hot is the sun? Isn't it like twenty or forty thousand degrees or something like that?" Brian asked.

"Well, the surface is only about ten thousand degrees. But the center is about twenty-seven million degrees."

"Holy shit!" Jessica covered her mouth only exposing her blushing cheeks, "Sorry," She said with a little smile on her face. She rarely cussed. "Why hasn't anyone else seen the white dwarf or whatever it's called?" Jessica asked.

"It's like Brian said…the government can give and take away information. You see," he looked to Jessica, "do you remember me telling you about SOHO," she just looked at him, "how about

Yohkoh?" she had the glazed over, deer staring into the headlights look. "Anyways," Mike looked at her with frustration.

"SOHO is the Solar and Heliospheric Observatory," Brian interjected.

"Nice," Mike was complimentary of Brian's knowledge, "It was launched on December 2, 1995 by NASA. It orbits the sun, balanced between the pull of the gravity of earth and the gravity of the sun. It continually monitors the sun and provides vital information to us."

"So when that dwarf star hits the sun, SOHO will be toast, won't it?" Jessica wondered.

"Yeah, literally," Mike responded.

"So, like I said, why hasn't anyone else found out about the dwarf star," Jessica asked again with skepticism.

"You see Jessica," Brian tried to take the conversation back, "We, the government, control what information gets to who…that goes for many things. We can shut down the media if we want! If National Security is at risk, you bet we're gonna do it. We have been intercepting the information sent from SOHO, since it's inception, and filtering out the information that we don't want to get out. It's simple! Now, let me get back to my story."

"Yeah, yours is much more exciting," Jessica replied, grabbing Mike's shoulder.

Brian continued.

Once the public was convinced that survival was possible, The President would have them. The key was to have a plan that sounded successful no matter how futile it may be. The President needed the American's, as well as the world's, buy in. The government didn't want the people to know that most of the people on earth would perish; they needed to give them hope. If they had hope, many people would still work. The U.S. alone would need millions of people to continue working in order for others to survive. They would still need food, shelter, clothing, water, and a local government to monitor it all. If everyone gave up, all of humanity would quickly perish.

He would announce a plan to drop leaflets within twenty-four hours to the entire country that would have information on survival tips and where certain shelters were. In addition, he would inform the people where to go for supplies, including blankets and space heaters. The plan would also entail an executive order telling all retailers, from the largest chains to the smallest mom and pop stores, to distribute all necessary food, water and supplies necessary for people to survive. Each person would receive supplies necessary to help cope with the weather. All companies would be reimbursed by the government for all supplies furnished, plus twenty percent, which would be repaid within thirty days. At least they would think.

Next The President would give instructions to all law enforcement and military personnel to move into all major cities and impose a 9 pm curfew to all of the citizens.

Any person found in public, after the curfew, would be arrested on site. The National Guard would be called up immediately as well as all Military Reservists.

The government believed that The President's address to the nation would build stability and avoid any major rioting and all law enforcement and military personnel would be in place until the end. The hope was that other countries around the world would follow in the American's footsteps and impose similar instructions for survival on their people.

Brian explained that prior to the Presidential Address, the Commander-in-Chief would have a conference call with every mayor and governor across the nation explaining, in detail, what they had discovered, and fax all of them the Executive Orders on exactly what to do, and when to do it, to avoid any major incidents. The President knew that the key to avoiding complete pandemonium around the country was to convince all law enforcement and military personnel that everything was under control at the national level. And that it was up to them, at the local level, to keep law and order.

Mike knew that the instructions were merely a pipe dream as all of mankind would perish within a week, or so, of *Sun Death*. The only reason the government was disbursing them was to give everyone hopes of survival and to make it more believable to the public that they were all in this together.

But The President felt as though the government owed it to the American people. Moreover, there was a slim chance that the weather conditions wouldn't get too unbearable and people could survive...for a while. In addition, there was a minute possibility that the white dwarf star could miss the sun altogether. If that happened, *The Chosen* would sneak back to earth, avoiding public knowledge that they abandoned the people back on earth; left them for dead. So it was important for people to stay calm, cool, and collected.

Brian went on to explain that as all life on earth was slowly perishing, The President, along with *The Chosen*, would begin their journey to find another planet that would be inhabitable for human, animal, and plant life. All of the spacecrafts that the government had sent out to take pictures, and explore the Galaxy over the last few decades, were geared towards finding an inhabitable planet. Even if it took generations to find another planet, *The Station* could sustain itself.

The Station's power supply could sustain itself for an indefinite period. The government had found that the gases in space could actually be used to fuel the special engines needed to propel it through space. Brian used the analogy that it was like cars using the air people breathe as fuel.

"So *The Station* can run forever, without refueling?" Mike questioned.

"Exactly."

"But what about food and water and everything else people need to survive?"

"I'll tell you what…I have pretty much everything you could possibly want to know about *The Station* on disk and you can read it tonight. I want to tell you everything I don't have on disk, just in case something happens to me."

"What are you talking about?" Mike looked confused.

"Yeah, what do you mean?" Jessica sat up in the back seat.

"You never know. We're on the run and for all I know, they may think I am in on this. They probably figure that I will have divulged sensitive information to you by the time, we either get caught, or get to Washington. Who knows what will happen to me, but I want you to know everything just in case."

At that moment, Mike started to see Brian as more of a part of the team than an opponent. He knew that there was still a chance that he was lying to him, but if that was the case, why would he be telling him all of this classified information about *Sun Death*. He decided to roll the dice and gamble with trusting him with both his and Jessica's lives. Mike knew that if they worked together as a team there would be a much higher probability of their mission to the nation's capital being a success.

Brian continued.

The President would confer with Federal, State, and Local law enforcement daily. They would assume that he was still on the planet. Shortly after *Sun Death,* he would tell everyone that he had been relocated to an "undisclosed location" for his safety. He would tell that to the American public, but tell his subordinates, on earth, that he was staying at NORAD. This would be the most likely place The President would be taken if something of this magnitude took place-unless you've been building a space station for over four decades.

They made it safely to a hotel outside Little Rock, Arkansas and they were all exhausted. Mike wanted to nose around in Brian's laptop, but he was too tired. He would wait until the next night. The trip was going as planned...so far.

Chapter 9

The Station

They had made it safely out of Little Rock, Arkansas without any incidents or run-ins with the law. The day before, Mike's exhaustion halted any attempt to read the information on Brian's laptop, but he needed to learn everything. Even this day, he was dying to read it, but didn't know if he had the energy to. His body was screaming for rest and he didn't know how much longer he could go on. They were finding it harder each day to sleep, but their exhaustion this day, would make it easy. The stress from driving, constantly trying to avoiding any law enforcement, while making sure they abided every speed limit, was slowly pecking away at all three of them. Mike decided to stop just short of Raleigh, deviating from the original plan of stopping past the city. He was nodding off at the wheel as the others slept…and he had to read.

A cold shower was exactly what Mike needed to get a clear head and stop his eyes from crossing. The first few minutes of the shower were freezing, but his body and mind went numb. He started beating himself up inside. He thought, *What have I got my family into? Is it my fault that both of my children are dead?*

Mike wanted nothing else than to wake up from this nightmare of a life that he was currently living. He fantasized about waking up from this bad dream or escaping to a far, deserted island where he and Jessica could live in happiness forever, but that was impossible at this point. If they tried to fly out of the country, their names would be flagged in some computer and they would be arrested immediately. Mike jokingly reached over and pinched his left arm testing to see if he would wake up, but only felt slight pain through the numbness. He dropped to the floor of the tub, covered his face with both hands, and began to weep.

Mike hadn't cried that hard since Billy died and even then he didn't do it in front of anyone. He was an emotional man, even getting teary-eyed while watching movies with Jessica, but was embarrassed about doing it. But as he got out of the shower, Mike felt like he had just got a hundred monkeys off his back; he was refreshed.

"What the hell...Mike come out here, quick!" Jessica yelled from the room.

Mike swung open the door only to see both of them watching television.

"What? You scared the shit out of me!"

"Look," she pointed at the television screen.

"You're on America's Most Wanted. Bet you never thought you were going to be a movie star, did ya?" Brian was trying to break the tension in the air, but it was impossible.

"Honey, the man said you killed a policeman that was trying to arrest you and they have it on video! Is this true?" she looked concerned.

"What?...No! What do you mean, killed a police officer? What the hell is going on Brian?" Mike walked over to the TV.

"I think I have an idea, but lets see. That was just the introduction to the show...I'm sure it gets much better," Brian responded.

Mike was the lead story for the show. The host stated that Mike Collins was under investigation for espionage by the government, and law enforcement went to his residence to take him in for questioning. Upon entering his home, Mike knocked one of the officers out, which was the man that was with Brian, and struggled with the other man. Mike was then shown on video knocking a man to the ground, tying them both up and then shooting one of the men in the back of the head.

Jessica looked at Mike.

"Honey, please! It didn't happen like that...ask Brian," Mike looked to Brian, "tell her!"

"Jessica, it didn't happen like that. They are making this up to get all law enforcement in on the chase and get local residents to help them find us."

Mike pulled back the curtain just a bit to peek outside. He stared toward the office, which was directly in their view.

"Yeah, we're really going to have to watch what we do now...where we go...who we talk to, everything!" Mike said.

After some commercials, the show went on to say that after Mike shot the officer, he kidnapped his boss, Brian, and then hooked up with Jessica for a getaway.

"They're making us look like Bonnie and Clyde, this is ridiculous!" Mike was astounded. It looked so real on TV; the way they portrayed Mike...the fake video. It made Mike replay in his head what actually had transpired that day to ensure that it really didn't happen like that.

"Mike, remember when I told you that the government can influence people into believing anything they want? This is just one small, minute incident of it."

"This is ridiculous...look!" Mike gestured again at the television.

Again they showed all three of them stating that Mike and Jessica were "armed and extremely dangerous" and that authorities were unsure of exactly what they were driving. The show stated that they were probably taking Interstate 70 toward Washington D.C. and they may be trying to inflict harm on The President himself or conspire with other terrorists.

"This is the most ridiculous thing I have ever watched!" Mike was in awe. He was furious. "They just showed me shoot some man and now they're saying I'm a terrorist and might try and assassinate The President! Unbelievable!" Mike sat on the edge of the bed, head in hands. "Maybe we should just turn ourselves in. Everybody is going to be looking for us now…we don't have a chance!"

"Yeah, maybe we should," Jessica agreed.

"Mike, look, don't let this get you upset. We have to stay focused on getting to Washington and meeting with The President," Brian interrupted.

"I don't know. Someone has tried to kill me! Now I'm on America's Most Wanted! What the hell are we going to do? We can't be seen in public, we're toast!"

"Look, we may or may not be, but lets get to The President and find out," Brian stood up. "We can let this get us all depressed, or we can let it push us to move on and achieve our goal…you decide!" Brian exclaimed.

Mike didn't think that Brian was a great leader, but he did know that he had the ability, though not used much, to say the right thing at the right time to motivate people. The difference this time was that he wasn't acting selfishly for his own personal gain. He seemed to really want them to get to Washington.

Though Mike was upset with being on national television, he did learn some vital information from the show. It appeared that Mike's plan to take a southern route to Washington was a success. Also if the government had any idea of what they were driving, they would definitely have put it on the show. In addition, Mike's picture wasn't very recent. Mike's picture showed him clean-shaven, and he had a beard now, and looked completely different. Mike hoped these points would work to their advantage.

It was almost midnight and both Brian and Jessica were asleep. Again, Jessica gave one of her pain pills to Brian so he could rest; they were getting addicted to them. It was the only way they could rest. Mike longed for some sleep, but he was too stressed. He couldn't afford to take any medicine that would affect his awareness while he was sleeping; he was a light sleeper, waking at even the smallest noise or movement of the bed. Mike didn't enjoy it, but on this trip it worked to their advantage and one of Jessica's pills would ruin it.

He decided that it was time to start nosing around in Brian's laptop and learn about *The Station* and hopefully more about *Sun Death*. Mike wanted to know everything; the more he knew, the more of a threat he was and he wanted the upper hand with the people in The White House. He had vital information to share with The President, that he hadn't even divulged to Jessica…and wouldn't. He was too afraid that if they were captured, or if any number of scenarios happened, she may compromise the mission; not intentionally, but potentially.

Mike was astounded by most of the information regarding *The Station*. It was a vast vessel, resembling spaceships shown in futuristic movies. *The Station* had one thousand different living quarters and could support that amount of people, plus the crew, for an indefinite amount of time. The quarters ranged from studio apartments to lavish five bedroom homes. As Mike looked through the information, it was set up like it was a vacation package. People could browse through information regarding each type of quarters with all kinds of details from type of tile in the bathroom, to what name brand of refrigerators each residence had. It was obvious to Mike that this was information that was only given to *The Chosen*, so they could see and pick the type of living conditions they were going to spend the rest of their lives in.

The propulsion of the spacecraft was phenomenal. As he learned from Brian, it would convert the gasses from space into fuel to propel the twenty-six engines that were larger than the Space Shuttle's; they had five hundred thousand pounds of thrust each. *The Station* could cruise at ten thousand miles per hour, which was unheard of on earth, and required only ten minutes to attain. It was slower than a space shuttle, but it was also much, much larger.

Mike quickly stopped and went back to the living quarters.

"Why are there over one thousand living quarters and there are only four hundred of *The Chosen* being evacuated?" Mike whispered to himself.

He couldn't figure it out. Even though an extra six hundred people wasn't a large amount compared to the three billion people that were going to perish during *Sun Death*, it was still a number almost double what the government was going to evacuate. This baffled Mike.

The computer showed that there was a crew of approximately fifty, which would service the entire ship. They included mostly what was described as *Base Level Functional Positions* for the spacecraft. Pilots, engineers, facility maintenance, food preparation, etc. There would be several hundred other positions, but they would be filled with *The Chosen.* The fifty staff had been chosen in 1999 and they came from all parts of the country. What Mike found interesting was the way they were chosen.

The government started looking at prospective people to fill these positions in 1996. They had specific physical and mental requirements. Each person had to have an IQ above 125 with a 4.0 average in both high school and college. In addition, there couldn't be any family history of mental illness. Next, they looked at physical characteristics. Each person had to be completely healthy with no history of any illnesses other than the common cold. Furthermore, there could be no history of family illnesses for the previous one hundred years. If there were any exceptions to any of these requirements, they were taken out of the pool of possible candidates.

They took all of their information from national databases. They sent out questionnaires to several colleges across the country that year asking for all of the information on both mental and physical aspects of each person. Little did the people know when they were filling them out, that they were indirectly applying to be saved from *Sun Death.* Of fifty thousand questionnaires sent out, the government only received seven thousand responses. Of those, they would only choose fifty people, but before they were chosen, they had to meet additional criteria.

They had to be between the ages of twenty and thirty years old and fertile with no transmittable sexual diseases. Background checks were done on each person to ensure only the most reputable people were chosen to continue the human race. They had to establish that they had work ethic by showing a good work history. Lastly, they had to show that they were financially responsible. If their debt to income ratio was too high, they were denied. All of this data was submitted, calculated, and evaluated by the government without each person knowing why they were giving out their personal information. They were told it was just research conducted by the government.

The most interesting aspect of the hand selecting was that they were chosen without them even knowing. Once a person was chosen, they had no choice as to what was going to happen next. As *Sun Death* approached, and various positions needed to be filled on *The Station*, the government systematically kidnapped each person and shipped them up to space. Once up there, they were debriefed about *Sun Death* and that they were chosen to survive. They had no choice...they had to live with the fact that they were chosen to continue the human race.

What if they didn't want to stay up there? Mike thought. He quickly found the answer.

By February 2000, all of the Base Level *Chosen* had been sent to *The Station*. Of course, upon getting there, many of their feelings differed. Some were happy to be a part of what they considered an elite few. Others were saddened by the fact that their friends and family members were going to perish, and they never had a chance to say goodbye. Others were upset that they weren't given the choice as to whether or not they even wanted to take on the responsibility of continuing the human race.

All of them had one thing in common; they weren't given a choice. It would have been too difficult to keep *Sun Death* a secret with so many people on earth knowing about the end of humanity. It could compromise the escape plan and National Security. The government had to make a decision and live with it. Therefore, any person not wanting to take part in the survival of mankind, up in space, was given the choice of death by lethal injection or could be sent back to earth after *Sun Death*. They had no other choice.

Who the government chose to go to *The Station* was one of the topics that Mike was the most obsessed with because of how difficult, or easy, it must have been for the government to choose a person to be saved from *Sun Death*. He couldn't imagine being in the position of choosing whether a family, or a part of a family, would survive, while others would perish.

Each living President, along with a spouse and two children were automatically accepted. All of the other *Chosen* were at the discretion of The President and Vice-President in office at the time of *Sun Death*. Mike found it extremely outlandish that The President would personally hand pick these people. Something about it didn't sit right with Mike; it was extremely prejudiced. He had to look for other information...something less serious. He clicked on "History."

Construction began in the early 1950's on the vast project shortly after the government learned of *Sun Death*. They put their top engineers and scientists together on the project. They turned Area 51 into not only a holding facility for the damaged UFO, but a construction facility for *The Station*. It was built in twenty-foot sections, and shipped up into space. The Space Shuttles alone flew eighty-one missions from April 1981 to January 1997 to and from *The Station*. Of course, they had other, less significant, objectives to accomplish during their flights to appease people on earth, but those were forged by the government to hide the truth. It would take until some time during the year 2006 for *The Station* to be fully operational.

Mike had always been fascinated with cloning and when he saw the icon underlined, he had to click on it. Cloning had been underway since 2000 on *The Station* and they were still working on perfecting it. This meant that, once perfected, they would have an endless amount of meat for the residents, all the scientists had to do was create them from samples of DNA. Mike found it very interesting that the government brought strands of DNA from every existing animal, from earth, along with DNA from every extinct animal they could get their hands on.

Also aboard the ship were most types of livestock. The pictures showed cows, pigs, chickens and many other animals that would be processed into food. The information showed that an actual USDA inspector would be on board to ensure that all meats were processed in an appropriate manner and to ensure all health regulations were adhered to. Mike was astounded as to how well planned *The Station* was.

All of the animals were kept in an area of *The Station* appropriately called "The Farm," which was on the opposite end of the vessel from the living quarters. The Farm, which Mike thought looked more like a zoo, was enormous. It wouldn't be fully operational until at least ten years after *Sun Death* due to its complexity. Most areas of The Farm were like a zoo exhibit. Some areas were only twenty feet by twenty feet and a few others were a half-acre.

The government planned to have the more popular species of animals cloned, after *Sun Death*, and put back into a simulated natural habitat on *The Station*. There wouldn't be any duck billed platypus', but just the basics to re-create earth and most of its natural inhabitants. As Mike read on, he learned that the purpose of The Farm was to try and make the long journey on *The Station* more enjoyable for it's residents. It was also a great resource for future generations in the event no inhabitable planet can be found.

Mike was astounded to find that the government wasn't even sure that there was a planet out there that humans could survive on. As the information continued, he saw another icon that said "Resident Agreement" and he clicked on it.

Upon reading the Agreement, it was more of a contract. It entailed that *The Chosen* were under the same Federal and State Laws as on earth and had to abide by them. There would be no prison on *The Station;* only a few holding cells. It was expressly stated in the contract that if any person was found guilty of a charge that required prison, they would be sent back to earth in one of the evacuation pods. What Mike found interesting about the pods was that there was a notation on the bottom of the page that released any responsibility to the government. It read that the evacuation pods were meant for a temporary escape from *The Station*, and not intended to enter the earth's atmosphere. It also stated that it had not yet been proven that a human could survive the heat generated by an evacuation pod entering the earth's atmosphere. So it would most likely be a death sentence.

All *Chosen* had the responsibility of providing a service or duty to *The Station*. For example, if an FBI agent was chosen to go up, Mike read, he may be employed as an investigator or in law enforcement. There would be a full law enforcement division as well as two Judges on *The Station*.

Mike was amazed as he read all of the positions they were going to need up there. Farmers, butchers, scientists, attorneys, teachers, a complete medical staff, etc. Every person would be used for some vital role on *The Station*.

There was too much information for Mike to read in one night; it was time to rest. Moreover, the three of them were about to embark on the final leg of their journey and they had a long day ahead of them. It was a short ride to Washington, but also the most dangerous. The government knew they were coming, just not from which direction and there would surely be a larger law enforcement presence as they approached the nation's capital. Mike prayed that luck would be on their side, but he knew it would take more than that.

Chapter 10

The Meeting

They finally started their last leg of the journey...Raleigh, North Carolina to Washington, D.C. All three of them were completely exhausted from the trip, but the adrenaline of having less than five hours of traveling left, was their caffeine for the evening. There wouldn't be a need to stop at Starbuck's to jump-start this day.

They hopped on I-85 North and headed to Richmond, Virginia; it was one hundred and twenty three miles away. Then all they had to do was jump on I-95 North and it was a straight shot to the nation's capital.

All three of them knew that even though they were close to their destination, the rest of their mission wouldn't be a walk in the park. There had been many close calls and near misses with the law, but luck had been on their side...so far. They hoped for the same in Washington.

"Brian, I told you this would be a piece of cake," Mike said as he laughed.

"I had complete confidence in you Mike," Brian responded with a little sarcasm.

"Yeah, right," Mike laughed, then looked at Jessica, "what are we, about an hour outside Richmond…honey?"

"Um…hold on, let me look on the map…yeah, about an hour," Jessica was the navigator for the day; Mike was driving. They had come up with a job for each person on the trip; there was no free ride on this journey. One person, usually in the back seat, was the navigator. The person in the passenger seat was the lookout; they had binoculars and night vision goggles to look at oncoming vehicles and traffic ahead of them. The driver's main focus was abiding by every law-proper signals, lane changes, speed, etc. One traffic violation could potentially ruin the whole journey.

"Oh, shit!" Brian exclaimed as he was looking ahead.

Mike and Jessica saw it at the same time; it was a roadblock. There had to be about five cop cars and every car traveling on the road had to stop. There wasn't much choice, Mike had to act fast. The police positioned it perfectly; it was just over a hill and there wasn't much time to stop. When Mike pulled the Escalade to the side of the road, it was in plain sight of the police. If they turned around, it would be a sure sign that they were guilty of something and they would be chased.

"What are we going to do?" Jessica questioned.

"Well, we're screwed. We can't go through it, they'll recognize us…if we turn around, they'll chase us…so I guess we'll have to…" Mike didn't finish his sentence.

He hit the accelerator and headed off the road. They were heading straight toward the woods, hoping for a clear path. They found a dirt road and Mike started to see police lights behind him. They were far back though, the cars were having a much more difficult time than their Sport Utility Vehicle. They drove for what seemed to be about five minutes and the police lights were gone. He still had to drive as fast as he could since there would be a huge law enforcement presence in the area as soon as the word got out. Mike shut the headlights off.

"Oh shit! It's a helicopter!" Jessica yelled. The area around them was illuminated.

Mike was driving very fast, and when he leaned forward to look up at the helicopter, the spot light blinded him. He sat back, tried to focus on the road, but couldn't see anything. Before he could hit the brakes, the truck hit a small mound of dirt to their left and it catapulted them into the air. As they flew through the air, the SUV tilted sideways, and landed on the passenger's side. It was a violent crash, but Mike hadn't lost consciousness; the airbags ensured that.

Mike looked over to Brian, who wasn't as fortunate; he was unconscious. A moan quickly brought Mike's attention to Jessica. As he turned, she also had blood on her face, probably from hitting the side window.

"Honey, are you alright?" Mike asked.

"My leg...oh, my leg!" she moaned.

Mike quickly checked Brian's pulse and it was strong. He jumped into the back seat and looked at Jessica's leg. It wasn't a pretty sight...it was a compound fracture, with at least one leg bone penetrating the skin; there was a lot of blood.

Sirens could be heard far off in the distance and the spot light from above was searching for them. They had gone off the dirt road, maybe twenty feet, and the trees were too thick for the helicopter to see them. The light was on the road, right where they headed off. The people in the helicopter were signaling the location of the truck, and the police would be on top of them within minutes. The sirens were getting louder.

"You're going to have to go without me!" Jessica said.

"I can't!" Mike responded.

"If you don't, we're all going to get caught!"

"I can't just leave you here!"

"I can't move...there's no way we could make it together...go!" She leaned her head back and moaned again.

"No!" a tear ran down Mike's face. He knew he had to, but he couldn't muster up the courage to admit it.

"God damn it, go! Get to The President...then come and find me!"

"I love you," Mike caressed her face and kissed her on the forehead.

"I love you too. Just make it all worth it, Mike! Don't let them win! Do it for Billy!" then Jessica screamed in pain and laid her head back again.

"I'll do it for all of us," Mike responded caressing her cheek.

Mike grabbed a bag out of the back and his gun out of the glove box. He climbed out the driver's door, which was quite difficult with the truck on its side and gravity working against him. He pushed the door open, then it quickly slammed. Mike looked through the window, not being able to see Jessica with the darkness and the window tint. He pointed his index finger toward where she was, and tapped on the window, "I'll find you, I promise!"

Mike jumped off the truck and headed deeper into the forest. He couldn't walk, he had to run; the sirens were very close. The lights from the police vehicles could be seen through the trees in the distance. Soon, they would be hot on Mike's trail.

As Mike ran away from the crash site, he couldn't help but struggle with his decision to leave them, but he knew that if he was captured there might never be a chance of him meeting with The President. There were now at least two helicopters in the area and more sirens could be heard off in the distance getting louder. They were coming from all directions.

The woods were thick enough to give him cover, but not too thick to hinder his movement. Mike knew that it would be nearly impossible for any helicopters to see him through the dense trees and would use it to his advantage. Nevertheless, he had to find a safe haven before daybreak.

Mike's biggest concern was how he was going to make the final stretch to Washington. He still had about two hundred miles to travel, and he didn't have transportation. Off in the distance, he could hear vehicles traveling, which meant that a road or highway was near. He stepped up his pace a notch to make it to the edge of the trees to see what was in his path.

In front of him was a highway, probably I-85, extending in both directions. Mike had lost track of where he was and before he went any further, he had to pinpoint his location. Remembering the contents of his bag, Mike crouched down and pulled out a map and a small flashlight. Turning his back to the highway, he illuminated the map and tried to estimate where he was. Using a compass, he figured out which direction he needed to head. Mike wasn't much of a woodsman, and never did much camping with the family, but over the years of working with the government he had learned a few things about survival.

Before Mike's last project in South America, he was required to take some survival training, which included self-defense and weapons training. Of course, had Mike known of the requirements before signing the contract, he would never had taken it; his training meant it was a military project which he tried to avoid. He had learned not to set expectations of a project until he actually was debriefed on what it entailed because many times it would be much different than he thought; as was the case with *The Collin's Project.*

By estimating approximately where they had headed off I-85, and guessing how far he had traveled on foot, he figured that the stretch of roadway in front of him was the same interstate they were on, before coming to the roadblock. Mike had to head north if he wanted to make it to Washington, but he had to figure out how. He could hear sirens again to his left coming down the highway, then they appeared and disappeared to his right.

He concluded that there were only two options for him and both had their own risks. The first was to follow the highway, on foot, and maybe steal a vehicle at a rest stop. Mike knew that there would soon be law enforcement and dogs on his trail and he was no match for them at this point. The other option was to try and hitch a ride, preferably from a truck driver, to Washington. After pondering on it for several minutes, he decided to try and hitch a ride and hope for the best.

Standing on the side of the road was the riskiest part of this option. Several police had passed by just a few minutes earlier, and here Mike was, standing on the side of the highway, waving at truck drivers as they drove by. He was also concerned that an unmarked police or government vehicle may come up on him without him even knowing. But luck was on his side, and it only took about five minutes to get a truck driver to stop.

"Good morning to ya!" A thin bearded man opened the passenger's door and welcomed Mike into his truck.

"Good morning. Thanks for stopping!" Mike had never said something so sincere in his entire life. They started down the highway.

"Where ya headin'? My names Bobby, what's yun's," the man had a strong southern accent that Mike wasn't used to.

"Yuns?" Mike repeated, hoping he wouldn't offend the man.

Then a head popped out from behind them and responded, "He means yours," then she slapped the driver on the shoulder, "You know I'm just messing with you Bobby."

She appeared to be a teenage girl who looked nineteen at the oldest. She had blonde hair, brown eyes, and was very beautiful. Mike sensed that she wasn't Bobby's daughter, and was probably a runaway that he had picked up on the road.

"Um, my name's John...John Smith," Mike couldn't think fast enough to come up with something less peculiar.

"Well, John...where ya headin'?" she responded, "Oh," extending for a handshake, "I'm Angel."

"Pleasure to meet both of you," Mike shook her hand. "I'm heading to Washington. Is that where you two are heading?" Mike was hoping for a confirmation.

"Yeah, this here's my last stop, ya know, Washington that is," Bobby stated.

"Yeah, then we're heading to Niagara Falls, right Bobby?" Angel asked.

"That's right darling! So what are yuns doin' out here in the middle of BFE, John?" Bobby asked.

"Well, my car broke down a few miles back and I thought I could hitch a ride the rest of the way...I'm in a little bit of a hurry."

"Hurry, what fer? You headin' away from those police back there," then Bobby looked at Angel and they both laughed; Mike had to join in so that he didn't look guilty.

"Yeah, I saw all of those cops. What the heck happened back there?" Mike asked, trying to act ignorant.

"Well, we heard that a wanted man, Mike somethin' or other, pulled his car over to the side of the road and killed his wife and a man he had kidnapped. They said he was armed and dangerous," Bobby looked over to Mike as if waiting for him to say something.

"Yeah, when Bobby saw you on the side of the road and said, 'hey, let's stop and pick this hitchhiker up,' I said, 'are you crazy, that could be that psycho killer guy,' and he said 'yeah right, what are the chances of that?'"

"Yeah, what are the chances?" Mike responded not knowing what to say.

"What are you goin' to Washington for?" Angel questioned.

"I'm going there on business...anyways, how far are we from D.C.?"

"About fifty miles or so...we'll be there by morning. You tired, jump back in there and get you some shut eye. You look tired."

"I'm going to take you up on that Bobby...I'm exhausted!"

Mike was worn out and wanted to end his conversation with them; he went to the cabin and laid down. All he could think about was Jessica and Brian and what had happened to them. He kept trying to convince himself that he had no other choice but to leave them, but there were so many questions unanswered. This was the first time he actually thought of what had transpired in the last hour and it overwhelmed him emotionally.

Mike awoke to the force of the semi stopping, which nearly rolled him out of the bed. He had fallen asleep and couldn't believe how rested he was. Mike felt uncertain as to what had transpired over the last six hours and was hoping that it was just a nightmare. The stench of dirty laundry and body odor quickly gave him the answer, as he realized he was in the back of some guy named Bobby's semi truck, with some teenager, that might be abducted; he could be an accessory to that also. That thought quickly exited Mike's head as he thought of his poor wife and what she may be going through at that very moment. He had to get to The President, and soon.

"John, this here's the last stop. If yuns need to shower or see a man about a horse, now's the time. Man, I think I have a turtle head poppin' outta my ass," Bobby seemed distinctively blunt and not embarrassed to say the unthinkable.

"Thanks," Mike couldn't believe what was transpiring. The thought of calling the police and giving himself up quickly popped into his head, then disappeared; the public wouldn't find out about *Sun Death*. The government would get ahold of Mike and make him disappear off the face of the earth-quickly.

After showering at the travel center, Mike decided to make a quick phone call to The President. He knew that it was risky, and they would trace the pay phone, but he had to set up a time to meet with him.

"This is Mr. Rotin."

"This is Mike Collins, please let me talk to The President, and fast or I'm hanging up!"

No more than two seconds later, "Mike, where are you? You're in a lot of trouble, you better turn yourself in."

"I need your promise that if I come to meet with you, you will sit down and listen to me."

"Okay, when?" The President asked.

"Today, 5 p.m., and I'll come to you at The White House. And I'm not joking, I have documented everything and if a certain person doesn't hear from me daily, the information I have about *Sun Death* will go to all of the media."

"I told you about mentioning that on the phone."

"I don't give a shit! And my wife better be alive, and well and I need to talk to her before we talk. Deal?"

"Deal."

Mike hung up the phone, jogged out to the semi, and they headed for Washington. He would have Bobby drop him off outside the city; he didn't want to discuss where he was really going and why. He also realized that once they traced the call to the truck stop, the government would be looking for him, and semi trucks would be their first choice.

The truck was dead silent after they left. Angel was in the back putting on tons of makeup and periodically popping her head out asking for Mike's approval of the results. Mike needed their help, but he was scared to ask; he had no choice.

"Look, Bobby and Angel...I need your help on something. I know we haven't known each other for that long, but I need a favor."

"Okay, what is it?" Bobby looked more confused than ever, so Mike turned to Angel.

"Look, I need a phone number where I can contact you tonight, tomorrow night, and so on. If I don't call you, I need you to call this number," he handed her a piece of paper, "and tell the person on the other end that Mike, I mean John," hoping they hadn't caught him slip out his real name, "didn't call you last night. Okay, this is the important part...tell him that Plan B has commenced and that, if he doesn't hear from you tomorrow night, proceed with Plan C."

"Plan B, Plan C, what?" Bobby repeated it, but was perplexed.

"Okay, John...Plan B has commenced, be ready for C," Angel repeated.

"Alright, so what do I need you to do...repeat it," Mike felt like he was talking to a couple of seven year olds.

Angel took control, "If you don't call us tonight, call this number and tell him Plan B has commenced and to be ready for Plan C if he doesn't hear from us the next night."

"That's it. Can you guys do this for me?"

"Yeah, but what's going on? You're not some sort of terrorist or something are you...like Al Qaeda?" Jessica asked.

"Do I look like a terrorist? Look, all I can say is that I work for the government and it's a matter of National Security that you do this. You will be serving your country. But here's the catch, don't breath a word of this to anyone...your lives could be in danger!"

"Your pullin' my tallywanker?" Bobby exclaimed.

"No, I'm not!"

Angel's eyes got huge, "Honey, look, you always said you wanted to be one of those FBI/CIA guys like Agent Mulder...here's your chance!" She was excited.

"Yeah, I reckon I kinda like the sound of Agent Bobby!"

"Okay, your country appreciates it. Look, let me off at the next exit, I will get a cab from there."

Mike didn't want to leave the security of traveling with two others and wished he could travel to Niagara Falls and forget about the world, but he had to find Jessica. He hated to think of what he would do if they killed his wife, but he had to plan for it. He knew that there would be no chance of him entering the White House with his handgun; if anything happened, he would be defenseless. But Mike was counting on having a calm, collected, and productive conversation with The President; he was counting on nothing happening to Jessica.

As Mike entered the Oval Office, he couldn't help but be more nervous than he had ever been in his life. The President was sitting behind his desk, with The Vice-President sitting on a chair in front of him. There were two other men, which were obviously secret service personnel, standing behind The President. They fit the typical stereotype of secret service men; dark suits, earpieces, and they appeared ready for anything.

"Good evening Mike," The President stood up and extended his hand. "It's a pleasure to meet you...I'm glad this whole fiasco is over."

"Yeah, I have a few questions about that sir," Mike wanted to know who was trying to kill him, "but first, I want to talk to Jessica!"

"That'll have to wait a bit, Mike," The Vice-President interjected.

"Actually, no! I want to talk to her right now!"

"Relax, we can get her on the phone," The President responded, "Look, she wasn't in any danger of dying in the accident, was she?"

"That's exactly my point! She was fine yesterday, and she should be fine now. But someone tried to kill me when I talked to you the other day on the payphone, remember? When I called you outside Amarillo?"

"Mike, we don't have any idea what you're talking about," The Vice-President again was getting between the two of them.

"Look, I'm talking to The President...not you! Now did you, or did you not, send someone out to kill me the other day Mr. President?" Mike demanded.

"That's completely absurd," The President exclaimed.

"Then someone else," Mike looked at The Vice-President, "is up to some things that you need to be aware of."

"Could all of you excuse us, please?" The President looked at everyone but Mike.

"Jim, I really don't think..." The Vice-President quickly responded.

"I'm not asking you to think right now...go!" The President demanded.

"Alright...but I warned you that this guy's nuts," The Vice-President shook his head as he walked out.

Mike could sense that The Vice-President felt threatened by Mike and wanted him to keep his mouth shut. He thought that it was possible that The President wasn't aware of some of the things that were going on; The Vice-President might have ordered the hit on Mike.

"Look Mike, I'm not sure what's going on, and why you kidnapped Brian, if in fact, that is what happened, but…"

"Please, let me talk to Jessica!"

"Alright, but she's fine," he reached for the phone and dialed. "Yeah, it's me…yeah…uh huh. I don't know, but he wants to talk to her. Yeah now, put her on! Mrs. Collins, Mike would like to talk to you."

"Honey, are you alright?" Mike asked.

"Yes, are you?" she responded.

"I'm okay, how's Brian?"

"They said he didn't make it."

"What? How? Are you sure?" Mike looked at The President.

"Mike, he seemed fine when they took him in the other ambulance. I mean, he had a concussion, but hold on," she was now talking to someone else, "alright…hold on…just a few more seconds…look…let go!" she was yelling now.

"That's enough, she's fine," a familiar voice said, and the phone hung up. He had heard the voice before, but couldn't put a face or a name with it.

Mike hung up the phone and turned to The President.

"Alright, are you happy?" The President said, "I told you she was alright. Now, let's get down to business. What caused you to go crazy, kill a man, take your boss hostage, all the time trying to reach me? What do you have to tell me that's so important?"

"You do know about *Sun Death*, right?" Mike asked.

"Of course I do."

"And you do know that I've been working on *The Collin's Project* for ten years?"

"Yes."

"Then are you familiar with those bastards killing my son?"

"I'm familiar with the accident. It was a real shame and I'm sorry, but it's ludicrous to imply that he was killed! Why would they kill him?"

"To shut him up…he had just found out about *Sun Death* and was heading back from spring break when they did it!"

"Who are they?" he appeared to be a brilliant liar or an ignorant President.

"I don't know. It's you...they...it's all the same to me! All I know is that the evidence I uncovered proves that someone killed my son and Jessica lost our little girl. I couldn't even tell her that it would have been a girl or she would have surely killed herself! We just want out of the project and our exemptions!"

The door opened and The Vice-President quickly entered the room.

"This is absurd! Why are you even listening to this? I told you he was crazy!"

"Richard, what do you know about Billy's death?" The President demanded an answer.

"Look, Jim," Richard was standing next to The President. He lowered his voice to a whisper.

"I don't care about that, did you, or did you not, order it?" The President was getting perturbed.

The Vice-President whispered some more, and then The President told him to leave again.

"Look, Mike...is what Richard told me correct? Did Billy find out about *Sun Death* and then possibly try and compromise the Project and National Security?"

"I don't know for sure, but it's possible," Mike knew the answer, but didn't want to say yes.

"Look, sit down...we need to talk. Would you care for a drink?" The President walked behind his bar.

"Sure...do you have Brandy?"

"Of course, it's my favorite...on ice?"

"Please."

"Look, Mike...as you know, we have known about *Sun Death* since the '60s. You are the fourth, highly talented scientist to confirm the results. All four times at least one family member has tried to compromise the Project."

"And what happened to the others? Did you guys kill Sukami?"

"Mike, that's absurd. You have been watching too many conspiracy theory movies. Sukami, and his family, are all doing well and are already on *The Station*. Please let me finish. In the event that there is a leak, the supervisor on duty sometimes has to make decisions very quickly to save the project and neutralize any National Security risk."

"So they just decided to kill my twenty-four year old son?"

"It was a tragic accident! Richard has informed me that they apparently tried to stop him, and as a result of the pursuit, he was killed. My apologies go out to you, and your family, for your loss, but we couldn't let him compromise the project! The public cannot, and will not, know about *Sun Death*! Do you have any idea, any idea at all, what would happen if the general public knew that the world was going to end? Do you?"

"What?"

"The police would stop showing up for work! The military would stop serving their country! Most people would stop showing up for work! I mean if people stop paying their bills, who's going to kick them out of their homes, repo their cars, risk their own lives, when the world is going to end? Within a few weeks, people would begin not caring about their future and repercussions of their actions! Crime would escalate to uncalculatable levels...murder, rape, you name it! Within weeks most, if not all, law enforcement would have quit or had to quit due to the threat of continuing to try and stop the lawlessness! There would be no government! Why would people care enough to continue working or serving their Local, State, or Federal Government if those very people were abandoning them? If the public found out that we could only save several hundred people and they were stuck here to die, to burn to death, they would come in herds to try and escape! It would ruin any chance for our survival! Do you see where I'm going? I haven't even got into what the rest of the world would do! Many hostile countries would use it as their chance to try and attack the U.S. just in case *Sun Death* didn't happen! We have it all figured out! We have a committee of specialists that can pretty much forecast how humans, all around the world, would react under these conditions!"

"Well, Mr. President, I never looked at the big picture like that, but there's still are a few things that are troubling me."

"Like what, Mike?"

"Like, why are we only sending up four hundred people, plus staff, when *The Station* can hold over a thousand?" The President looked surprised.

"I'm impressed! You have done your homework. Brian said you had read pretty much everything on his laptop. Look, it's not easy choosing who is going to live and who's going to die. Do you think I enjoy playing God? I don't...I have nightmares almost every night. But I always keep in mind that we finally have a chance to start over up there," he pointed up, "We humans have really messed up this earth, especially us here in the United States. If you look at what our founding fathers intended this place to be and look at it today...it's a joke. Our kids can't say The Pledge of Allegiance in school. Everyone's suing everyone. We have politicians that screw everything up. Our government is so corrupt, and screwed up, that the best thing that could ever happen is for us to start over! We are hypocrites; we build nuclear weapons and then tell other countries they can't! The U.S. is slowly taking over the entire world! We are the police of the world. We are imposing our beliefs on the rest of the world and they are either for us, or against us. Mike, I'm going off on a tangent that I really didn't intend to do!"

"Mr. President, you haven't answered my question. Why are you only sending up four hundred people instead of a thousand? And I still want to know who was trying to kill me?"

"I'm sorry, this Brandy goes right to my head. Mike, I'm going to look into that because I didn't know anything about somebody trying to kill you. But what I will tell you is that I had nothing to do with it, you have my word on that! Now as to the capacity of *The Station*...look, four hundred, or one thousand, what's the difference? There are billions of people on earth!"

"Yeah, but you could save six hundred more people. Your goal should be to save as many people as possible!"

"My goal is for the number of people, I decide to save, to live comfortably and safely on *The Station*. We are behind on the progress of it being finished and I can't compromise the lives of four hundred people by adding more. When *The Station* is fully operational, it will support a thousand, but it's not ready yet."

"But from what I read, it is about eighty-five percent operational now. So the math would suggest that about eight hundred and fifty people could be on board."

"Look, I think you have bigger things to worry about than a few hundred people surviving," The President was changing the subject,

"The committee is going to meet tomorrow regarding your exemption with everything that has happened."

"What are you talking about?"

"I'm saying that now that you are in custody, the committee has to decide what is going to happen with you and Jessica's exemption from *Sun Death*. Do you have anything to say in your defense? Why did you kill that man back at your house?"

"I didn't kill anyone! That was made for that show on TV! Brian even admitted that they staged that to get state and local law enforcement to step up their efforts toward capturing us!"

"Well, I'll have to make a few phone calls, but at this point it still stands that you have killed someone and cost the government vast time and effort with this whole ordeal. And to talk to me about what? Brian mentioned that you had to talk to me, and only me, about vital information regarding *Sun Death*."

"That is the second time that you have mentioned that Brian told you something, both after our crash! Jessica said that she was told that Brian died!"

"He did die! He had a blood clot in his brain after the accident, but before he passed away, he was able to talk with some agents and did give them some information."

"I don't know what to believe anymore!" Mike stood up, "Who's alive...who's dead...what the hell's going on! Are you saying that Jessica and I may not be taken care of with all of the hard work I have done for you guys over the years?"

"Everything you have done, doesn't mean anything, Mike, if you killed someone. The guidelines are simple regarding *The Chosen*."

"I told you, I didn't kill anyone!"

"Well that remains to be seen. Now what did you uncover about *Sun Death*?"

"Nothing...nothing at all!" Mike decided that he wasn't going to help the people that had sent his son to an early death and was about to do the same to him and Jessica and billions of people across the globe. He just had to come up with a quick lie to appease The President.

"Come on Mike...we know you have discovered something! I'm sure we can work something out." The President looked directly into

Mike's eyes. "Tell me what you uncovered and you can count on being on *The Station*."

Mike could tell he was lying. "Really, Mr. President?" he was playing the game.

"Yes, I promise."

Mike decided that he was going to give in…at least The President would think. He was going to give them some bogus information and see what would happen to him and Jessica. If The President lived up to his word, he would then give him what he had actually uncovered about the end of humanity.

"Well, first of all, I wanted to tell you this personally because I felt that my life and Jessica's were at risk. So I wanted to get here, tell you what I have found, and then tell you that I really want out of the project!"

"Yes…go on." The President slid to the edge of his chair. Mike had his full attention.

"Well, I want to tell you, but I'm concerned…"

"Tell me Mike!" The President was getting impatient.

"Just a little information to help with the evacuation. I found that Dr. Sukami's calculations were a little off. I'm pretty sure that *Sun Death* will take place about twenty-four hours earlier."

"That's it?" The President sat back in his chair. He stared at Mike in disbelief, trying to read whether he was lying. Mike kept a straight face and maintained eye contact with The President.

"Well, it's a big deal if your one of the last to go up and I assumed you would be! And I wanted to make sure that you personally got this information. With all of the weird things going on, I had to make sure you knew. Twenty-four hours could mean life or death for you, Mr. President!"

"I appreciate that Mike…I'll tell you what…with the whole manhunt ordeal, we are going to have to take you into custody. Of course this is just for the media. We will have you arrested and I'll have a word with the judge. We'll have you out on bond in a few days."

"And Jessica?"

"She's already in custody in a military hospital."

"Is her leg alright?"

"Yes, and a few bumps and bruises. She's just there for observation after what happened to Brian." Mike felt that The President was holding something back…not being honest with him. Mike had no choice but to go along with the plan.

"Richard…come on in." The Vice-President came in looking at Mike as if he wanted to physically hurt him.

"Is it time to take him in?" Richard gestured toward Mike.

"Yes. Let's do it like we planned. I told Mike what's going on."

"When will I hear from you Mr. President? We didn't finalize a few things."

"We'll take care of it in a few days…now go along. Let's get this all over with." The President started to pour himself another brandy as the two secret service men, along with The Vice-President escorted Mike out of the Oval Office.

The four of them went downstairs and one of the men handcuffed Mike. As he peered out the window, he could see several police cars outside with their lights on and assumed they were there for him.

"Wow, we're really going to make the media believe this." Mike looked to The Vice-President.

"They're going to believe it alright." The Vice-President said with an evil tone.

"Look Richard, I'm letting you know that if anything happens to me…"

"Oh, your going to make threats now?" he questioned with confidence. A confidence that whatever Mike had to say didn't matter. It seemed that Richard thought he had the upper hand.

"No, I'm just letting you know that if anything happens to me…if I don't call someone each night, the media will know everything!"

"What did you do…give some truck driver, and his little bitch, your contact number? Real smart!"

Mike was flabbergasted. He thought *How in the hell did they know he did that? These guys must be everywhere! This is ridiculous! How did I get into this fucking mess?* He was speechless.

"What's wrong…the cat got your tongue?" The Vice-President said.

"What did you do to them?" Mike questioned.

"Don't worry about it! You have bigger problems." The two men led Mike outside towards a black van with tinted windows-two police cars in front, three behind.

He could tell he had obviously angered The Vice-President and that didn't fair too well for Mike. Richard F. Delong had retired as head of the CIA about fifteen years earlier and had a bad wrap as a dirty fighter. Mike had several conversations with Brian regarding Richard, and nothing positive was ever said. Brian reported to a man, who reported directly to Richard, so they obviously knew every move of Mike's during *The Collin's Project*. Brian told Mike several stories of people crossing Richard, who vanished from the face of the earth; he knew he might be next. It would be easy for Mike to disappear now. Who would look for him?

As they left, Mike wondered *What should I do? Richard has it out for me...I'm screwed. I need to do whatever it takes to get out of this mess. I need to just kiss his ass, apologize for everything I've done wrong, and hope he'll spare my life.* He felt like he was talking about a King or a mob boss.

Before the White House left Mike's view, he turned around, glanced at it and smirked. He hadn't really told The President what he had uncovered about *Sun Death*-Mike was holding the trump card. He thought *We'll see who has the last laugh!*

Chapter 11

Plan B

Three days had passed since Mike had been brought to his cell. Nobody had came to see him, question him, talk to him-nothing. He was beginning to wonder what their plans were for him. After leaving The White House, he was transported about an hour south to an undisclosed location. Shortly before getting there, he was blindfolded so he wouldn't know exactly where he was being taken. When he asked about Jessica, they wouldn't answer. He had been sitting in the four-foot by six-foot cell like a prisoner of war.

Mike couldn't believe the loneliness of being in captivity. He wasn't sure as to where he was, but he was sure that it wasn't the average jail; probably a military holding facility for people like him. There were other cells in the building, but they only totaled twelve and he was the only prisoner. The walls were cold and solid steel with no windows to see what was left of the sun's life. He had a cot, a toilet and a sink…that was it. Not the Marriott like he was used to when away from home. A single guard stood outside the door of the small building, and Mike would periodically yell to him to see if there had been any word from The President yet. The guard would open the door and peek his head in. He would then grin at Mike, shake his head and chuckle like *A fat chance in hell you crazy son of a bitch! Maybe the president of the koo-koo's nest!*

Mike decided that enough was enough and he was going to raise hell if nobody came to talk to him the next day. That day came and went with no visit. At supper when the guard brought him his food, he took the metal tray and flung it back at the guard.

"I want to talk to The President and I want to talk to him now! What the hell is going on around here? I have rights! I want to see a lawyer!"

"Look, someone is coming here next week!" the guard was really pissed off, mashed potatoes and gravy all over his chest, "but I'll tell you what, if you ever do that again, so help me God, I'll kick the shit out of you!" The guard was trained to kill and Mike could see it in his face. He was built like a freight train, and there would be no stopping him. He appeared to be in his early twenties, probably right out of boot camp. He seemed hard on the outside, but Mike knew that if was going to be in there a long time, he would have to dig to try and chip away at it. Hopefully to find a man inside that would help him. But he had to start now.

"Look man, I'm sorry. But I'm about to go crazy in here! I have no idea where my wife is! I'm in jail like some freaking criminal! The President promised I would be out in a few days! All this, after busting my ass for decades for this government! That's gratitude for you!"

"I don't know what to tell you man. All I know is that at fourteen hundred hours, next Wednesday, someone is coming to see you!"

"Who? What day is it?"

"It's Monday and all I know is that my Sergeant said I better have my boots spit shined come next Wednesday, or I'd be cutting potatoes all week. Must be someone important."

"Maybe The President? This Wednesday or next?"

"Next. And I don't know who's coming. Why are you always mentioning The President like he's a friend or something? Is it for real or are you some looney bastard?"

"They probably told you I'm crazy, but I'm not. Look kid, I've been working on top-secret projects for this country since before you were born." Mike knew he should stop burning the bridge he had lit with the mashed potatoes. Mike always hated it when he was younger and people would say "before you were born" to him; he changed his tone. "Look. I'm not crazy. I'm an everyday, ordinary person who just ended up on the wrong project at the wrong time. I really am sorry about the food...maybe you could just come talk with me periodically if I'm going to be in this shithole for very long?"

"We'll see. But if Sergeant finds out, it'll be my ass...better not for now."

Several days had passed and Mike was getting to know the evening guard, Chris. He would come inside, out of the night, and talk with him periodically about current affairs and what was going on out in society. The young man was just as Mike had hoped, hard on the outside and a softy in. But it would take much work in order to gain his trust enough for Mike to use it to his advantage.

It was Friday night and Mike couldn't fall asleep. He wondered *Who is coming to see me next week? Where and how is Jessica? What is going to happen to both of us? Would The President live up to his word? How am I going to get out of there?*

Each night he was brought a couple of pills, which the night guard would say would help him sleep. He was scared to take them; he may never wake up. That night, he was going to take the chance. There was no way he was going to be able to sleep so he popped one in his mouth with some water. He tried to relax. He tried to think nice thoughts of him and Jessica on a far away, exotic island, enjoying their lives. He fell into a deep sleep.

"Rise and shine! It's chow-time!" a familiar voice yelled.

"Huh? Chris? What the?" Mike felt hung over and could hardly focus.

"What's wrong, drink too much?" the guard laughed. Mike sat up, trying to regroup his thoughts wondering why Chris, the evening guard, who he was trying to befriend, was there in the morning.

"Man, I took one of those pills and I was out. But I feel like shit now!"

"Yeah, those things will kick your ass! You didn't take a whole one did you?"

"Yeah, what are they?" Mike wasn't sure if he wanted to hear the answer.

"I'm not sure of the name, but most people say it's better to only take half."

"What are you doing here in the morning? You were here last night."

"Yeah. But I left early. I finally got switched to days. Laura hates when I'm on duty at night and it just wasn't working out."

"Laura...aren't you two getting married in a few weeks?"

"September third."

"I was wondering what happened to you last night. Some other guy brought in those pills."

"Yeah...I told that bastard to tell you to only take half, but he's an idiot! Probably thought it was funny or something...he'd screw up a wet dream! We all call him Dipshit."

"Well, I second that! What's for breakfast...the usual?"

"Yeah, oatmeal. And it looks like scrambled eggs, I think. And some cold bacon, but the coffee's just how you like it."

"You're alright, Chris." Mike felt the opportunity and took it. "Look, have you seen my wife? I'm dying to know if she's alright."

"You know I can't discuss that with you. You're going to get me in trouble!"

"I know, but you've got to understand. What if you hadn't seen Laura for a week or so, what would you do? Just tell me if she's alright!"

"Well first of all, if I had killed someone and had every law enforcement agency in the country looking for me..."

"Is that what they told you? Come on, they didn't let you in on it?"

"On what?"

"On what? You've got to be kidding me...I'm not really being jailed. The President had to stage this to keep the media off his back. He was supposed to contact me in a day or two, but I'm sure he's busy. He *is* The President!" Mike was trying to convince himself more than Chris.

"Here we go again, hold on…" Chris was pretending to have a remote control in his hand, pointing it through the bars at Mike, "Oh, look what's on…it's the Looney Tunes, starring Mike!"

"That's funny, but keep your day job!"

"You keep talking about The President like he's coming to see you. From what I heard some lawyer is coming to see you, that's it!"

"Who told you that?"

"Just heard it through the grapevine…did some asking around."

"If it's just a lawyer, why do you have to spit shine your boots? Did you think about that? Someone is coming, and it's not some lawyer!"

"Alright," Chris seemed to be patronizing him and Mike didn't like it.

"Yeah, alright!" Mike wasn't the nicest person to be around first thing in the morning, and when he didn't feel well, he was downright mean. "Now let me eat my breakfast before it gets even colder!" Chris was walking away now and Mike was talking to himself, but wanting Chris to hear, "You figure you could at least let me have some hope if they're going to keep me in here."

Mike had to plan for the worst and hope for the best. Worst-case scenario, he was going to sit in the cell until *Sun Death* occurred. Planning for that, if anything positive came along, it would only help. His long-term goal, though it couldn't take too long, was to win over Chris, who would help him get out. The only problem was that one day, Chris could be gone and he would have to start over with another guard, which would take time; Mike had to work quickly.

The next Wednesday came and a lawyer did show up to meet with Mike. Mike wasn't sure what to do so he didn't say anything about the world ending-not yet. If he did that, it could possibly compromise his escape. If he did, the lawyer would tell the prosecuting attorney, who was probably hired by the feds. Then The Vice-President would find out; Richard would probably just have him taken out back and shot.

Mike sat there listening to all of the charges the government was filing against him. From second degree murder, to assault with a deadly weapon. From transporting illegal firearms across state lines, to kidnapping. The list went on and on. They were going to build a case against Mike that he couldn't defend. Mike was still hoping that The President could, and more importantly, would get him out of this. If not, Mike would probably end up in a prison cell next to some man who would try and make him his girlfriend. After speaking with the lawyer, they came to the conclusion that the only way he would get leniency would be to plea temporary insanity.

Mike wasn't even concerned with the lawyer or the case against him. He had a much bigger plan, and it included him escaping; Chris was the key.

"I told you it was some lawyer," Chris quickly pointed out after he left. "But I do have some good news. That wasn't the important person that was supposed to come. Actually," he toned his voice down just above a whisper, "The Vice-President was supposed to come down here, but I guess there was some suicide bomber that blew himself up in Israel so he had to meet with The President or something."

"Where do you get your information?" Mike was heading down another road. He wanted to see what kind of connections Chris had.

"I know some people in Washington," Chris responded confidently.

"Like important people or grunts, who overhear things?"

"A little of both."

"Is Richard still coming?"

"Yeah, I heard tomorrow."

"Look…just do me a favor. When he's in here with me, keep the door open a little or leave that little window on the door open a crack, and listen. You'll see that what I'm saying is for real. Once you believe me, I can tell you some things that will knock your socks off!"

"Your gonna get me court marshaled!"

"No I'm not. Trust me, just do it and you'll see."

"Alright. Look, another thing…I overheard a couple of MP's talking and it looks like your wife's fine. I think she's pretty much in the same situation as you. I mean, she's in solitary confinement, but she's in Building Two on the other side of the complex."

"Man, you don't know how much that means to me! I'd appreciate it if you could keep your ears open, just in case anything happens to her."

"Not a problem, but if it ever comes up, you didn't hear it from me."

"I know. Trust me, I've been interrogated many times and it takes a lot for me to crack."

"Cool. I figured as much being Mr. Top-Secret and all," Chris had a big smile on his face.

"You'd be surprised at what I've done for this country over the years. Projects that you probably couldn't even imagine. Projects all over the world."

"Yeah…tell me one."

Mike went on to tell Chris one of the Projects he took in the Middle East that had to do with Sadaam Hussein and biological weapons. It wasn't a really exciting Project, but he knew it would hook Chris. He was using Chris's fascination with Mike's job as bait to reel him in. Before long, he would gain his trust, but Chris had to eavesdrop on Mike's conversation with The Vice-President; that was crucial.

Mike's nervousness the next morning was overwhelming. He felt like the meeting with The Vice-President would pretty much decide his fate; at least from Richard's point of view. He figured that Richard's plan was probably to keep Mike locked up until *Sun Death*, then Mike wouldn't be an issue at all. Mike's plan was to quickly feel out how the conversation was going and then, if it wasn't going well, try and get Richard to say some things that Chris would be flabbergasted over. Now was his chance.

As Mike heard the door to his building open, he looked up to see one of the same men that were in the Oval Office, walking toward his cell. Next Richard walked in, and finally another suit.

"Mike," Richard said, "Are they treating you alright?"

"Yes. The only complaint I have is that I'd like to see Jessica," Mike responded looking to see Richard's reaction. Mike wanted to see if it was even an option.

"Look, Mike…after consulting with several of our staff, including The President, we have decided that it's National Security's best interest to keep you locked up until *Sun Death*."

"I'm going to have to stay in here? And then what? Am I going up to *The Station* with everyone?"

"That remains to be seen...we haven't decided on that yet. Look at the bright side...would you rather be in a big prison, in solitary confinement, or this plush, little known, holding facility like this?"

"Why wouldn't we be able to go to *The Station*? After all of the hard work..."

"I don't give a damn about all of your hard work! Do you know how hard I work? And I have to watch my parents die down here in a few weeks! None of us chose to be in this situation, we're just in it and we all have to deal with it! All of the hard work you have done doesn't mean shit now that you've fucked up *The Collin's Project*!"

"That doesn't answer why I might not be saved?"

"Mike, I assured people that *The Collin's Project* wouldn't be a disaster and you and Jessica managed to turn it into one! To be honest with you, I really don't think you two deserve to be saved!"

"So I'm going to be a prisoner here until *Sun Death*?" reality had smacked Mike right in the kisser.

"Yeah, that's the bad news. The good news is that we are going to move you down two cells...to the large one, and Jessica can come in here with you."

"You're serious?" To Mike, all of the bad news suddenly didn't matter.

"I wouldn't joke about that."

"When can I see her?"

"I don't see why you can't start tomorrow. I'll talk to a few people."

"So, level with me...is there any chance of us going to *The Station*?" Mike pleaded.

"After everything that has happened...I doubt it. You take care of yourself," Richard headed toward the exit.

"You too...Dick!" Mike said. He knew Richard hated to be called that. He knew he shouldn't have said it and it could even of cost him his life, but he had to get one last punch below the belt in.

Mike was fuming and wanted to go off on The Vice-President since he first opened his mouth, but that would have been a foolish thing to do. He was still trying to play his cards right; make people believe that he had given up. Make people think that he wasn't a threat. Mike had his poker face on and he was hiding a Royal Flush, but he had to be able to show his hand.

About five minutes after Richard left, Chris came in and walked down to Mike's cell.

"What the hell just happened?" Chris exclaimed. He was staring past Mike in a daze.

"Were you listening? The door was closed...and the window too!"

"Yeah! I planted a microphone down here," he walked down three cells, reached around a pole and peeled off some tape concealing a bug, "I could hear everything through my earpiece...didn't want to draw any attention by trying to peek in the door and listen. What the hell did he mean by *Sun Death*? I'm going to have to play that all back. I think I missed most of it cause I was in shock."

"You crazy son of a bitch! You're lucky they didn't see that!"

"Yes...yes...and yes," Chris responded. Mike gave him a confused look.

"What?" Mike had no idea what he meant.

"Yes, I'm crazy. Yes, I'm a son of a bitch. And yes, I'm lucky they didn't find it."

"And what do you mean...play it back?"

Chris pulled out a micro cassette recorder that he had used to record the conversation with Richard.

"Are you nuts?" Mike exclaimed, reaching through the bars for it.

"What?" Chris jumped back, just out of his reach.

"What? I'll tell you what! If those bastards find out that you know about this, you won't have to worry about being court marshaled, they'll kill us! Make us disappear off the face of the earth!"

"How the hell are they going to find out? I'm not stupid! I might be young, but I'm not stupid!"

"Look, these guys are smart. They probably planted a microphone in here and are listening to us right now!" They both stopped and Mike checked around his cell while Chris spent about five minutes searching the building.

"There's nothing here Mike...you're just paranoid."

"Yeah. You would be too, if you were in my shoes! Like I was saying, these guys are everywhere! If they didn't plant one yet, I'm sure they will! I suggest that we only talk about things outside. When we have our thirty minute walk and stretch."

"Whatever you say man."

"Trust me on this one! Hey, see if you can find out when Jessica's coming down here...would you?"

"Yeah, but you didn't answer my question...what the hell is *Sun Death*? And he was talking about you two dying down here...and you said something about going up somewhere or could you go up there, with them, or something!"

"Look, I don't know if you're ready for this yet, but I'll tell you a little. And I'm not kidding when I say that you can't breathe a word of this to anyone! Not even Laura...not yet! You will be able to tell her soon enough if you help us get out of here. I have a plan that can save all four of us, but it'll only work if you follow my plan to the T; no deviating, no improvising! Do you understand?"

"I think so...I mean, yes I do! But I don't understand what's going on!"

"I know...it's confusing. But I can't tell you everything yet! Here's the deal," Mike lowered his speech to a whisper, "You help us get out and I'll have a place for us to go. Then I will tell you everything including how we'll survive *Sun Death*."

Mike went on to explain briefly what was going to transpire over the next month. When Mike was finished, Chris looked as though he was under a spell.

"So let me get this straight," Chris caught how loud his voice was and whispered, "You're saying that the world is going to end in a month? Some white dwarf, or whatever you called it, is going to collide with the sun and destroy humanity?"

"That's it in a nutshell."

"And you want to escape out of here, with my help, risking my life...and Laura's too?"

"There's really no alternative if you think about it; come on, you heard Richard yourself! You know about *Sun Death*! You know now that I'm not some crazy son of a bitch! I didn't make this shit up! Chris, think about it...if we succeed, we can live! If we fail, we'll probably die! But if we don't even try, *Sun Death* kills us anyways! Do you want to be in control of your own destiny? You figure the odds! Fifty/fifty, zero…and zero! I'll take the fifty/fifty…what about you?"

"Fifty/Fifty is a lot better than zero…I'm in, but I want to help with the escape plan! I know this place better than you."

"Perfect! But when we decide on something, we stick with it; no deviating. First things first though…I need to see Jessica."

The next day Jessica was brought in and they were moved several cells down to a larger one. They spent the first hour embracing each other and crying. Her leg was in a cast and it was difficult for her to move around. Once they got acclimated to being together, they began to talk more. But Mike let her know from the get go that there would be no talking about *Sun Death* unless they were outside. They had checked for bugs in the building, but Mike had to be sure.

Their new living conditions were much better than Mike's original cell. Instead of giving them two cots, somebody hooked them up with a full-size mattress, though not in the best condition. It smelled like someone else, someone dirty, but it was better than a cot. The cell also had a small shower in the corner, which would be much better than the supervised bathings the next building over; they were in the honeymoon suite.

Three lengthy weeks had gone by with Mike and Jessica living in the ten by ten cell. Jessica's depression had set in and it was worse than ever, but the medication helped. She had to take three pills a day, with weekly physicals from a military doctor. She was diagnosed with clinical depression, but one good thing did come out of it. The doctor ordered that she needed two hours a day outside in the sunlight instead of thirty minutes. He said that that would help her more than the medicine. Mike thought, *How ironic that the one thing that the Doctor prescribed to help her depression the most, was what was depressing her in the first place.*

But Mike thought it was great. They were permitted to go outside and walk around for a two full hours. Jessica didn't have to wear shackles, her leg was in a cast from the knee down and she required crutches to walk. The exercise area was small and surrounded by razor wire, twenty feet high. However, they were able to move freely and stretch and do other exercises to help them survive the elements of captivity. More importantly, it gave them more time to plan their escape.

It was August 28, 2005; just ten days before *Sun Death*. They were going to escape in a few days. The plan was foolproof. On Friday, September 2nd, a few hours before his shift ended, Chris would slip some laxatives into George's coffee. Not just a little, but a lot. George was the night guard, and they needed him to be sick. Chris would offer to stay and cover the shift as he knew they already ran on a skeleton crew at night.

At midnight, Chris would unlock Mike and Jessica's cell and drop two .45 caliber handguns off to them and a pair of bolt cutters. Chris would then go do his walk around to show that he was doing his job. During that time, Mike and Jessica would slip out the front of the building. Chris had popped the one hundred watt light bulb that had been illuminating the outside of the front door, so that nobody could see that the front door would be open for a few moments.

Chris told Mike that the compound was actually very small, only engulfing about an acre. It was an abandoned Army Reserve station that hadn't been used in years until The Vice-President took it over. It consisted of four buildings and some equipment outside. Only two men were on duty at night. One walked the outside and the Sergeant on duty who usually stayed inside the main barracks watching television. All they had to do was keep the Sergeant from finding out, and they could be long gone come morning.

Once outside, Mike and Jessica had to move quickly to the south, away from the main barracks. This would alleviate any chance of the Sergeant stepping out front and seeing something since his door was on the north side. The plan was simple: cut a hole in the fence and walk over to the street where Laura would be waiting in a car for all three of them. It wasn't like getting out of Alcatraz, but to them it felt like it.

Their escape was flawless. As the four of them drove away from the compound, they knew they were fugitives and law enforcement would be looking for Mike and Jessica within hours. Mike exclaimed, "I can already see it on the news: *And our top story tonight, Mike Collins, the man who lead law enforcement on one of the largest manhunts in U.S. History a few weeks ago, has struck again. Him and his wife, Jessica, kidnapped a Military Policeman,*

*Private Christopher Atkins, and they are presumed armed and dangerous...*Laura, did you get this car from where I told you to?"

"Yes, just like you told me. I called that number you gave me and he set it all up. He said everything's legit and made sure it had a tune up." She reached for the glove box.

"He also said that these would come in handy," she handed an envelope to Mike, "new ID's and passports...just in case."

"You know Chris, that was an ingenious idea bringing in that disposable camera for these," Mike said as he showed the pictures to Chris.

"Every once in a while, I have a good one. Where are we heading?"

"I'm not sure," Mike responded, "Laura was supposed to tell Mr. X what I wrote down and everything was supposed to be taken care of...did you?"

"Of course. There's a map and directions to where we're heading each day in there. He also said there are some supplies, and a few toys for you Mike, in the trunk."

"I love toys," Mike knew that Mr. X, whose real name was Xavier Ramirez, would hook him up...and he did. They pulled into the hotel and drove right to their room. Mr. X already had keys for up to six hotels, if necessary, in the glove box. Each room was prepaid for two weeks, which would give them plenty of time before *Sun Death*. Also in the bags were hats, fake mustaches, bleach, fake scars and just about anything need to change a person's appearance. In addition to that, there was an arsenal of weapons and equipment.

"Okay, Mike...we got you out. Now tell me what's going on and what we are going to do!" Chris asked once they were inside the room.

"Man, you didn't waste any time!" Mike responded.

"Can we talk about this in front of Laura?" Chris asked.

"Might as well. As long as she doesn't freak out," Mike was now directing his words to her, "Look Laura, this is going to be a huge shock to you..."

"Yeah, I'm still in shock that Chris convinced me that we had to break you out, and that it was a matter of life and death for us!" Laura responded with confusion. "What the hell is going on?"

"Mike, let me start it out," as Chris walked over to Laura, knelt next to her chair and grabbed her hand, "Look, first of all, you have to trust us on this. I know Mike is telling the truth. I overheard The Vice-President of the United States confirm it in front of him…so it's true! But anyways, please don't freak out when I tell you this. Mike has assured me that everything will be fine if we stick to his plan."

"Okay, you're scaring me now! What is it?"

"In a few days, a white dwarf star is going to collide with the sun causing a thermonuclear explosion. The heat will char most of humanity. The oceans are going to boil away and earth's atmosphere will deteriorate. Most of humanity is going to die and it's called *Sun Death*."

"What the hell are you talking about?" she stood up, "A dwarf what? This is bullshit! We broke them out for this?" Laura exclaimed.

"Shh. Look we have to keep it down," Mike interjected; he had worried about this moment.

"What's going on Chris? What are we going to do?" Laura questioned; she sat down and began to cry.

"Relax, trust me. The government has plans for some people to be sent up to a space station to survive it!"

"And are we going?" Laura quickly questioned with hope.

"I don't think so, but Mike has a plan so we'll survive."

"What's the plan?" she looked to Mike, then Chris did the same.

"First of all, Laura, you have to trust me on this. I have been working on a top-secret project near Area 51 on this for almost ten years. I know pretty much everything about *Sun Death* and the government's escape plan. We ARE going to be a part of the survival of this-trust me!"

"Yeah, but if we're not going up, how?" Laura was weeping, mascara running down her cheeks.

"It's really simple. All we need to do is follow my instructions and everything will be fine. But first and foremost, we need to all lay low until tomorrow. Laura, I need you to go to the store and get everything on this list," Mike handed her a piece of paper, "This should be more than we need to get by. Laura, did Mr. X confirm the time of the meeting with the news guy outside The White House?"

"Yes," she could hardly talk, "It's…" she was shuffling through a notepad, "Yeah, 7 p.m. on Sunday, September 4th like you asked."

"Okay, today's Saturday the 3rd, so we have one day to prepare before the meeting and two days before *Sun Death.*"

"Chris, I'm scared," Laura whined. Chris sat next to her and put his arm around her.

"Just relax, it's going to be okay," Chris said.

"We need to lay low, and then Chris and I will meet with the news crew. I need both of you," looking at Laura and Jessica, "to stay in the room and monitor the police scanners and CB radios for any unusual activity or anything that shows that they're on to us. Next, Chris, did you contact your friend…the one that's a guard at The White House?"

"Yes."

"And what did you tell him?"

"That he had to trust me on this and that we would be out there at 7 p.m., on the 4th, with a news crew. I had to tell him a few things though."

"A few things about what? What did you tell him?" Mike stood up shaking his head in disbelief.

"Relax! He wasn't going to help us because he said he would lose his job. All I told him was that I predicted that The President would have a speech from the Oval Office, and that he wouldn't even be at The White House. I said that he was going to announce something and that once he heard it, and realized that The President wasn't even there, he would want to help us."

"That's it?"

"Yes, that's it."

"Well, just so you know, this is going to make this even more dangerous. I hope you can trust that guy! If he breathes a word of this, or once he finds out that you are missing and were either kidnapped or in on the escape…do you think he'll tell someone?"

"No, I told him that I was going to do something and that National Security was at stake and regardless of what he heard, to just trust me no matter what."

"How well did you say you knew this guy?"

"We grew up together...from grade school on up. We've been best friends for like fifteen years! I know him better than anyone on this planet and we can trust him."

"I hope so...for our sake. We'll have to make sure before we both commit to the final phase with the news crew...but we can make this work. Trust me, during the Presidential Address things will fall into place."

"So what's going on with the news crew, Mike?" Chris asked. The other two slipped in a "yeah?"

"Look, all of you are going to have to trust me on this. Here's what we have to do to survive..." and Mike went on to tell them the rest of the plan. He had to convince them that they would survive *Sun Death.*

Chapter 12

Up, Without A Hitch

Before meeting with the news crew, all four of them had extremely important tasks to perform. Mike and Chris were scouting out The White House and surrounding areas looking for an entrance, as well as escape routes. They were also looking for possible positions where people might have lookouts in surrounding buildings as a precautionary measure. Mike was concerned about the guard at The White House. He didn't know anything about the man other than Chris was vouching for him-that would have to be good enough.

The girl's were in charge of packing all necessary supplies for Sunday, September 4th. This included all weapons, communication devices, clothing, disguises, food, and water for the day. The weapons resembled what a small squad of soldiers would prepare before a mission. They had machine guns, hand guns, grenades, knives, smoke bombs, binoculars, GPS devices and on and on.

Since all four of them were wanted by federal, state and local law enforcement, they had to wear disguises. Chris shaved Mike's hair down to a burr cut, and bleached it blonde. Mike wore a fake mustache that matched. Chris's hair was already blonde with a burr cut, but he let his beard grow. The picture the military had of him was taken on a shaven morning. Chris's face would grow stubbles before noon each day and his facial hair was dark; they darkened his hair to match it. His five o'clock shadow was more of a one o'clocker.

The girl's disguises were much simpler. They would simply have to put their hair up in a ball cap and wear sunglasses and plain clothing if they were out of the hotel room. Nothing spectacular, as they wouldn't be having much contact with anyone on Wednesday.

Mike and Chris sat on a bench near The White House. "Alright...the news crew is going to meet us there," Mike pointed at the corner just down from The White House, "And you will be positioned there, Chris" he pointed to a spot down the street a little. "You will stay in the car observing closely what is going on around me. If you see anything suspicious, anything at all, let me know immediately. I'll have this on," Mike pulled out his earpiece, which was connected to an expensive looking walkie-talkie. "We'll all have these on channel eight."

"Got it," Chris acknowledged.

Mike was curious as to how the evacuation process to *The Station* was going. He knew that just a couple of days before *Sun Death*, almost all of *The Chosen* would be on board. The only people that were supposed to be left on earth was The President, Vice-President, the head of the FBI and CIA and a few other members of The President's Cabinet. That's it.

That night, the four of them watched the news. The news reported that several Space Shuttles were taking off and landing each day. The report stated that NASA was having some serious problems with the International Space Station and that it was "vital" for materials and equipment to be taken up there immediately to repair it. Mike knew that each Space Shuttle that went up there had approximately twenty-five people on board that were part of *The Chosen*.

Mike wondered how *The Chosen* were reacting to the fact that they had to leave their friends and family members behind to perish…to burn to death. Surely there would be a lot of depression on *The Station* for the first few months as reality of what they had done would set in. So many people dying on earth, but they had been spared. Spared to spend the rest of their lives traveling through space, looking for another inhabitable planet. Another planet that man could slowly ruin over several thousand years.

What astonished Mike most about the evacuations on the shuttles was that it hadn't leaked to the public. NASA wouldn't even be aware that four hundred and fifty people would be evacuated, right under their noses, without them knowing. The information on Brian's notebook computer explained exactly how they were going to pull this off…

Of course, several of the NASA staff would be in on what was going on, but they would also be part of *The Chosen*. The rest of the staff would be oblivious to the people boarding the shuttles. The live video feed on the cameras, that record who is doing what and where, would be tapped into. A different signal, the one the government wanted the staff to see, would appear on their screens. It resembled a movie where the security guards are watching the video, but it wasn't really what was happening right under their noses…it was brilliant. All of the evacuations took place late in the night to make it even more difficult to see the loading of several dozen people from a distance.

The most important trip would be the last one though. The last shuttle from earth to *The Station* would have all of the most important people on it. If something were to happen to that shuttle, Mike thought that one of two things would happen. Either the people up on *The Station* would be a lot better off…or a lot worse off. He thought, *It would be a Catch 22; their screwed with them or without them.* But with people like Tony Bair and Prime Minister Sharon, and many other world leaders up there, they knew they would be fine if The President didn't make it up there. The government was risking losing so much to keep the world in the dark. However, if suddenly many leaders of the U.S. Government disappeared at the same time, it might create a scare or start a media frenzy. They had to do it this way.

Mike couldn't help but think what he could have done differently to not have put Jessica and him in this situation. Wednesday would bring either the beginning of their new lives together, or possibly their deaths. The thought occasionally crossed Mike's mind that Billy hadn't been killed in that fiery crash that night. Maybe the government just made him disappear; maybe he was waiting for Mom and Dad up on *The Station*. But that was a delusion and he knew it.

Mike looked at his watch: Sunday, September 4th 6:45 p.m. His heart started pounding and he could feel each beat in his temples. He pulled out his pocket TV, and tried to tune it into a local channel. Any would do, as The President's address would be seen on every channel. Suddenly, he heard it announced.

"We are breaking into your regularly scheduled program, to provide you with this bulletin!" Then the news anchor appeared on the screen. "Good evening, we have learned that The President of the United States will be addressing the nation and the world in about one minute. There are no indications as to what this is about, but our sources tell us that everyone should watch it! We have been told that he is going to address the nation from the Oval Office," he paused. "Ladies and Gentlemen…The President."

"Good evening ladies and gentlemen. I have decided to talk to you this evening as a man, a husband, a world leader, and more importantly a person. We have found that something very disturbing is going to happen in approximately twenty-four hours and we feel compelled to share it with you. Now I could sugarcoat this and make it not sound so bad, but I won't. I owe it to you, the people of this great earth, to tell you the truth and be straightforward with you. In about twenty-four hours, a small star will collide with the sun causing a thermonuclear explosion. This is going to cause some severe weather changes across the globe as the sun will eventually perish. But please do not panic! I repeat, do not panic! We have put a few processes in place to make it more adaptable for the people across the country. I immediately call all Military Reservists to active duty…please report immediately. I am calling all of the National Guard to duty…please report immediately also. I'm asking all local law enforcement to set a permanent curfew to help the people of this great country. This curfew is immediate and is for the safety of our great nation. The explosion will cause the sun to release more energy and radiation in one day than it normally would over one hundred million years. After this broadcast, please tune into your local news as information is being sent to them immediately regarding where and when you can leave your home to get the necessary supplies to make this more bearable. Plenty of supplies will be available at your local retailers, but don't go now. Again, you will be notified, by your local news as to which zip codes will go to which areas to get supplies. If you don't have television, and are listening to this on a radio, stay tuned as to where and when you can go locally to get supplies. We have made every effort, in the short amount of time we have known about this, to make this as bearable as possible. I will not lie to you though, I don't know how hot it will initially get and what the ramifications of this will be. Will people die...it is possible. We have already put the world's top scientists on this to discover the effects on our planet...and us. What is important is that all people of this great world work together for our common goal of survival. I believe that with this happening, it will only make our world a much stronger place to live. It will only make us a much stronger human race, much stronger and more diversified than ever. To the world, I apologize that I couldn't notify you sooner, but we had to look out for our nation's best interest. Again, to our great country, please stay inside, and start to prepare yourself, and your family for this. We must keep our chins up and our heads held high, as we are survivors and can overcome this obstacle. I will address the nation again tomorrow at this same time. God bless all of you. Goodnight."

Mike felt sick to his stomach. This man had the gull to lie to the entire world and he did a fantastic job at it. He was on *The Station*, addressing a dying world and made it sound like a captain that would go down with his ship.

Mike could see the news crew walking toward the corner where they were to meet. Nothing looked suspicious, but Mike was nervous. He was sitting on a bench down the street, watching for any signs of foul play. Newspaper in hand, Mike was trying to blend in with society.

"Chris, does everything look okay from where you're at?" Mike asked through a microphone on his collar.

"Yeah...but how about that speech? Are you sure we're going to be alright?"

"Just trust me. Focus on what we're doing. You already knew that the speech was going to happen. Stick to the plan...and you hear that Jessica and Laura? Trust me!"

"Famous last words! It was just different hearing it from him," Chris responded.

"Jessica? Laura? How's everything look from there?" Mike questioned.

"Everything's fine from here. Laura's a little upset after the speech like you said she would be. But she's going to be fine."

"I'm counting on both of you...don't let me down. I'm going to walk over toward the news crew. Chris, if anything weird happens I need you in here like a bat outta hell with that car to get me."

"Roger that."

"I'm going to leave my mic on so you guys can hear everything...just in case I'm not able to speak to you."

Mike started walking towards the men. He was about twenty feet away when he recognized one of them; the man with the video camera. It was one of the President's secret service from the Oval Office.

"Oh shit! It's a setup!" Mike yelled as he dove for cover. All three of the men reached for weapons, as did Mike.

Mike had managed to get behind a tree and as the bullets were flying by, a huge sense of betrayal came over him. Aiming his 9mm, he couldn't remember if he had cocked it, so he didn't take a chance. He peeked around the tree and squeezed off round after round until his clip was empty; he reloaded.

"Chris, where the hell are you?" Mike screamed. No sooner than he yelled, he heard the screech of the tires sliding. He looked up to see Chris slide the car between Mike and the agents. Mike thought he had hit at least one of the men; they didn't have any cover and were lying on the ground exchanging fire with him. As the car slid to a halt, Chris opened fire with a machine gun. The shooting paused for a moment and Mike looked around. Everything was in slow motion and he heard nothing.

"Get in!" Chris yelled.

The agents stopped returning fire and remained motionless on the ground. Mike could hear screams and could see people running in every direction; it was chaotic. As he stood up and took a step toward the vehicle, Mike and Chris made eye contact. Then they suddenly heard a sound from above.

"It's a helicopter!" Mike yelled as a cannon from above sprayed bullets at them. He dove onto the ground next to the car; there was no time to move. The bullets hit the ground, quickly heading toward Mike and their car. One round hit the asphalt, inches from Mike's head, which was buried under his arms. A chunk of the blacktop hit Mike's elbow; it was a sharp pain. The bullets riddled the car above him and glass and bits of metal rained down on Mike. The gunshots stopped and the helicopter passed, but was sure to return and fire again. Mike quickly jumped up and looked into the car. Chris had been fatally shot, as there wasn't much left of his skull. He opened the door and pulled him to the ground...he wouldn't want Laura to see his gruesome body; he didn't have time to reflect...he didn't have time to think. Mike had to get out of there.

Just as he squealed the tires and headed away from the helicopter, he could hear the gun sounding off again...it was so fast. He had never heard gunfire so rapid, and he hoped he could evade the bullets with the car. Mike knew that he needed to head toward people, as surely they would stop firing. As he turned the corner, there were people around and the bullets stopped; he had to find an alley. He knew that he had to ditch the car since all law enforcement would be looking for him in the blue four door.

Mike had parked a second vehicle in a nearby location he had to get to it fast. But first he had to quickly blend into the population without making a scene. Mike pulled into an alley and quickly exited the vehicle. He could feel the wetness of blood, from his neck to beltline, and had to get his shirt off quickly. Chris's blood and pieces of what he assumed were bones and brains, clung to the driver's seat as well as Mike's shirt and neck. As he opened the trunk, Mike remembered that they brought extra clothing if needed. He changed his shirt and grabbed a duffel bag that had some necessities in it.

The bag contained more clothing, a disguise, ammunition, including grenades and smoke bombs, a few military rations of food and a sawed off shotgun. The keys to the other vehicle were already in Mike's pocket and he headed towards the street. Mike needed to find out exactly where he was and which direction he needed to go. But first he had to talk to Jessica and Laura who were screaming for a response from him. He could hear them through the earpiece that had fallen and was hanging to his side.

Mike paused for a moment and thought, *Who double crossed us? Was it Chris's friend? They're going to pay for this! I need to get back to the hotel and quickly.* He knew that the longer he was out in public, the better his chance of getting caught.

As he got to the sidewalk, he saw pandemonium. People were scurrying around, trying to find a safe haven; some walking, others running. There were at least two helicopters in the area and he wasn't sure if they spotted his abandoned vehicle or him exiting it. There were sirens in the air and some were getting louder, others fading. He saw a police car coming down the street toward him. He quickly entered a Café.

"Good evening sir," a pleasant looking older lady greeted him.

"Yes, do you have a restroom?" he quickly responded.

"We don't have a public restroom, but are you staying for dinner?" she was too cute of an old lady to refuse and he needed the restroom.

"Sure, I guess I could use some food," Mike was hungry; he just hadn't had a moment to think about it. With all that had just happen, he was afraid he would regurgitate any food he ate. But he needed to get off the street.

"I can't believe you're hungry after what The President just announced. Did you watch it?" she looked scared.

"Yeah…it's crazy."

"Everybody's spooked. Even my cook and waitress left…but I love to cook. Let me show you to your table and show you where the restroom is."

"Thank you."

"Our special today is meatloaf, mashed potatoes, whole kernel corn and some biscuits for only $4.99."

"I'm really not that hungry," Mike responded.

"What, that doesn't sound good? It's all homemade!" She was looking at him with puppy dog eyes, trying to give him the same guilt trip his grandma would always use on him; it always worked.

"No, I'm sorry. That sounds great! But no gravy please," Mike needed to get to the restroom. He had his hand over his earpiece, but could still hear a voice screaming.

"No gravy? We make it from scratch?" she responded not knowing he didn't care. Mike hated gravy. She gave him that look again.

"No, really. But thank you," he wouldn't budge.

Mike headed to the restroom. He hoped the restroom was for only one person at a time, so he could have some privacy...he was in luck. After locking the door, he quickly pulled out the shotgun, made sure it was completely full of shells and dug through the bag. He found the GPS he was looking for and also pulled out another fake mustache-his had fallen off. It would be too late to put it on now without drawing suspicion from the people in the Café. He would wait until exiting to the street; Mike stuffed it into his pocket.

"Jessica? You there?" he whispered.

"Mike?" he heard a frantic voice on the other end.

"Jessica?" he whispered again.

"No. She's in the bathroom! She'll be right back! Is everything okay? You sound funny!" Laura sounded worried.

"I'm whispering. I really can't talk long. I'll be back as soon as possible, we ran into some problems."

"Mike," Jessica quickly jumped in, "we've been trying to get you for about five minutes. Is everything okay?"

"No. I can't talk long."

"Are you guys okay?" Jessica asked inquisitively.

"I'll tell you about it when I get back," Mike preferred to tell them face-to-face to help Laura cope.

"Where's Chris? Let me talk to him!" Laura had grabbed the mic back.

"Gotta go...I'll be back soon. Stay at current location. Over and out," Mike ended the transmission and turned the walkie-talkie all the way down.

Looking at the GPS, he could see that he was only a few blocks from the other vehicle. Traveling two blocks normally isn't a difficult task, but when cops and feds are everywhere, it can be quite a task. He knew they would be looking for a blonde man so he put a hat on-he also quickly put some blue contacts on and some sunglasses, even though it was close to dusk. Mike hoped the hat, blue eyes and a blonde mustache would help hide his identity if he crossed paths with any law enforcement. He headed back to his table, as he didn't want to draw any attention to himself.

"Why are you wearing sunglasses? It's almost dark," the lady stopped at the table, "You didn't have those on a few minutes ago. Did you?...Boy, I lose track nowadays. I swear I have Alzheimer's or something."

"No, I didn't have them on, but I feel a migraine coming on and these really help."

"Oh honey, I'm sorry for prying," she was embarrassed about even bringing up her memory, "I sure bet some gravy would help with that headache though," she pinched him on the arm and walked off.

Mike was famished and any person around could tell by how quickly he inhaled his food. He also finished a basket of biscuits. He knew some warm apple pie would be a great finish to a fantastic meal, but he was already stuffed. Mike didn't know if the food really was that good, or it was the fact that he hadn't had a home cooked meal in over three months; it was probably a little of both. He realized that if he was put in any position to elude the law by running, he would certainly puke up everything he had eaten.

It was almost eight o'clock and was mostly dark outside. Mike paid his bill and while walking to the door, slapped on his mustache. As he walked out the door, he pulled his sunglasses off and headed west toward the car. He could still hear sirens and helicopters in the distance, but he had to focus on just walking to the car-not too fast or too slow.

As he approached the corner where he would turn right and see his vehicle, he saw the reflections of lights off the buildings across the street; they were police lights. There was at least one police vehicle right around the corner where his vehicle was supposed to be.

Mike walked out to the street, waved to a Taxi driver to stop. He jumped in, and as he passed the intersection, he saw feds all over his car. He hoped that nothing could trace them back to the hotel.

"Jessica? Laura? Are you there?" he impatiently demanded.

"Yes. Where have you been? We're worried sick about you!"

"I don't have time right now! Pack everything up and go to the next hotel on the list! Don't leave anything behind though...nothing!"

"What's going on? You're scaring us!" Jessica questioned. She began to cry.

"Look. Everything will be okay. Just do what I said! Pack everything up and get on the road. Did you guys ditch the last car and pick up the new one?"

"Yes."

"Good. What kind is it and what color?"

"It's a Ford Taurus...and it's teal."

"Alright. Now do what I said! Quick, give me the name and address of the hotel you're going to...and the room number too," Mike was trying to hurry her.

"It's the Pinkerton Lodge...room one fifty three."

"Okay," he directed his attention to the cab driver, "Excuse me sir, do you know where the Pinkerton Lodge is?"

"Yes. Is that where you want me to take you?"

"Please," now speaking to Jessica, "Okay, honey. I'm on my way. Now hightail it out of there...I mean it!"

"Okay, but your scaring both of us!" he could hear Laura crying in the background which got Jessica started again.

"Over and out," Mike ended the transmission.

"What was that all about?" the cab driver asked. The man peered at Mike through the rear-view mirror.

"Oh nothing. I'm just in a hurry," Mike had to think of something fast; what the driver overheard must have sounded peculiar, "I'm doing one of those treasure hunts with the radio station. Did you hear about it?"

"Really?" the driver peered at Mike through the rear-view mirror again.

"Yeah," Mike responded with confidence, maintaining eye contact with him.

"Did you hear about that shooting at the White House?" the cab driver asked.

"No. What happened? Is The President alright?"

"Yeah, but I guess someone tried to take him out. Shot three of his men, dead!"

"Really?"

"Yeah, one of them is still on the loose. Six feet, one inch tall. Blonde hair. Brown eyes. It's all over the radio. Hope they fry the son of a bitch!"

"You got that right," Mike was agreeing with the fatal ending of his own life, if caught.

The driver pulled into the hotel, which was only minutes from where he was picked up, "That'll be seven-fifty," the driver turned to Mike.

"Here's a twenty…keep the change."

"Wow! Thank you, sir! You have a great evening!"

Mike walked to room one fifty three and knocked on the door. He turned around hoping to see a new teal Ford Taurus, but there wasn't one around. There was a bench a few doors down so Mike decided to relax for a few minutes. He heard the sound of footsteps slowly getting louder to his right and looked up.

He saw a beautiful blonde, with long hair, walking toward him. She had a short spandex skirt on and a matching top, no bra. She appeared to be a working girl for the country's oldest profession. As she got closer, she began to speak to him.

"You want to talk to me? Do you want to talk to me?" she said quickly. It was obvious to Mike that that was her phrase and her walking wouldn't be interrupted. He was sure that if he gave her the right answer, or the possibility of it, she would stop.

"Um…no. Thank you though."

"Suit yourself," she muttered as she passed him. She hadn't wasted a second on Mike, and that was her intention.

Mike couldn't help but look at her tight ass and legs as she walked away from him. He thought that if he was single, he might have taken her up on the offer. He thought to himself, *Hell I don't even know if Clyde would work right now with all the duress I'm under. I'd probably need a Viagra or two*, and he chuckled to himself. Mike had named his penis "Clyde" as a teenager, but didn't remember why.

Jessica and Laura pulled up and Mike quickly remembered that he was going to have to explain to Laura that Chris was dead. He quickly brainstormed *Should I just tell her he's dead? Maybe I could tell her he was captured? Yeah, that'll help, otherwise she'll freak out and possibly ruin our chances.*

He knew it was a cruel thing to do, but he couldn't compromise the mission. It quickly popped into his head that this situation was similar to when Billy tried to compromise *The Collin's Project*. What would Mike do if he thought Laura might compromise everything? He figured that he would have to stop her at all costs. He just hoped that the government tried to do the same; not kill Billy, but stop him. It wouldn't bring him back, but it sure would put his mind at ease.

Laura quickly jumped out of the car, not seeing Chris. Her eyes were gaping, mascara down her cheeks.

"Where's Chris?" she demanded.

"Let's go inside and talk about it," Mike said. They entered the room.

"Where is he? The police scanners said that one suspect was shot, but they didn't say his condition! Was that him?" Laura asked.

"Yes, they got him," he kept a straight face, but couldn't stare at her in the eyes for more than a moment.

"What happened?" Jessica questioned.

"Yeah, what the hell happened? Where did they take him?" Laura yelled.

"It was a setup...somebody narked us out! I don't know if it was Chris's friend or the news guy," he sat down and dropped his head into both hands, grabbing his hair with both fists, "I don't know what he hell happened! All I know is that those bastards started shooting, then I started shooting...I think we killed three of them. Then this fucking helicopter came in and started shooting the place up! It was crazy!"

"Did Chris get shot?" Laura's curiosity was boiling over.

"I don't know for sure...we were separated. Then he came in and put the car between the Feds and me. He saved my life! But then that damn helicopter came in and luckily I made it out of there."

Laura grabbed the remote control and pointed it at the television, "Maybe we can find something out on TV!"

"Look, don't believe what they say on TV," Mike was trying to lay it on so if they announced Chris was dead, she wouldn't freak out, "the government will tell the media to say whatever they want the public to believe," looking to Jessica, "You remember what Brian told us! About making the public believe anything they want...don't you?"

"Shh. Here it is!" Laura pointed to the TV.

They watched the report, "In a related story, two gunmen opened fire in front of The White House today, presumably to try and assassinate The President. One suspect was shot and killed," Laura put her hand over her mouth and began to cry again, "and the other one is on the loose. Apparently three, that's three secret servicemen were shot and killed it the exchange of gunfire. The police are asking the public to help find this man," a picture of Mike appeared on the screen, "Mike Collins, some of you may remember that he is the man that broke out of a holding facility, about two hundred miles south of here just a few days ago. He is also the man, who kidnapped his boss, a month ago, and led police on the largest manhunt in U.S. history. We'll have more on this story in a few minutes, now back to you..."

Mike shut off the television. "Laura, like I was saying, they want people to think he's dead...he's not. He was fine when I left!"

"Yeah, but maybe they killed him!" she was snorting as she cried.

"Look, there were people all around. There is no way they killed him...trust me." Mike felt awful for having to lie to her, but he could tell that if she knew, it would be the straw that broke the camels back. She would go into a state of shock and never come out. They still had to continue the mission.

"And how are we going to get him back?" she quickly asked.

"Give me some time...I will come up with something." Mike tried to sound confident, but didn't think he was convincing her.

"Where would they take him?" she demanded.

Mike was getting in too deep with the lie, but he knew all he had to do was buy some time until *Sun Death*. He needed her to hold on until then.

"I know exactly where...there is a holding facility in The White House. That's where they would hold him...in the basement!"

"Why would they take him there?" Jessica questioned. Mike could have killed her.

"Why...because it's only twenty-four hours to *Sun Death* and they don't have time to do anything else!"

"What are we going to do know? Who double crossed us?" Jessica wanted to know as much as Mike.

"I'm not sure, but we'll have to go to Plan B," quickly thinking, "Yeah, Plan B. We'll go back out to The White House after The

President addresses the nation again. That's when it's all going to go down."

"What?" Jessica questioned.

"Yeah…what?" Laura joined in.

"You'll see…tomorrow's Judgment Day!" Mike said in a vengeful, evil tone.

Chapter 13

Judgment Day

By the time all three of them calmed down, it was after 3 a.m. Mike had to sedate Laura with some of Jessica's sleeping pills for her to fall asleep; Mike realized he would need the same. As he laid in bed, the next day's events began to unfold in his head. In order for his plan to be successful, he had to play out all possible scenarios and how he would react to them. Mike was pretty sure of what would happen out in society once *Sun Death* occurred-The President explained it clearly. However, Mike was hoping that The President's speech wouldn't tranquilize the public into staying calm and relaxed. He would need them to do the complete opposite in order for his plan to be successful; he needed chaos.

That night Mike dreamt of his entire family for the first time in a while-the family that could have been. He saw himself standing next to his stunning wife and their two children. Billy was a little older in his dream, maybe thirty. Next to him stood a beautiful little girl, probably four years old. She looked similar to Jessica when she was a young girl. Long, sandy blonde hair, halfway down her back. Beautiful blue eyes and pale white skin. A smile that would make any parent melt and a personality to go along with it. Mike wondered why Billy had aged almost ten years, but she was only four. This family would never come to be and once Mike realized it was a dream, the children disappeared and Jessica and him were heartbroken and began to weep.

"Oh my God!" Mike heard. He couldn't tell if it was part of his dream or reality.

As he awoke, he could hear the television blaring an annoying anchorwoman's voice. As Mike sat up, he felt hung over; it was the pills. It was early morning and Jessica and Laura were already up watching the news; it was very early morning.

"What is it?" Mike questioned, rubbing his eyes. He thought, *Nothing will surprise me now!*

"There are people freaking out!" Laura pointed at the TV, "Now that the curfew is off...during the day, I guess they're supposed to be going to get supplies. But the news woman said that the people are supposed to be going by zip codes, and nobody's listening...look!"

As Mike looked at the television, he saw complete pandemonium. People were running in the streets, looting local stores. Police were trying to curtail the looters, but the crowds were too immense. Smoke floated in the air as an apparent attempt to use tear gas to deter the looters. Mike wondered where the footage was from and hoped it was in the nation's capital. The news anchorwoman mentioned that it was in Chicago and Mike needed the chaos to swell to other areas of the country.

The plan that The President had put in place to keep peace wasn't working; at least not in some areas. On the news they stated that there wasn't nearly enough supplies for each family; that was making people panic. The television showed people fighting inside and out of stores. The news was trying to convey to the public that electricity probably wouldn't be lost, but the uncertainty was there.

Next, the footage went to Philadelphia showing the same mayhem. Mike watched the footage of hundreds of people running in the streets...it was total chaos. Police and military personnel were trying to curb the pandemonium, to no avail. Next, it was on to Atlanta…still the same. It appeared that most of the panic started in the urban areas, but it was spreading. Mike quickly remembered Brian telling him that there would be more bedlam in those areas and that it was supposed to be contained there. Mike walked over to the window to peek outside; everything was calm…for now.

"This is exactly what we need. We need some anarchy!" Mike was trying to build confidence with the women.

"Why? This is crazy! It's starting to look like the LA riots!" Laura responded.

Mike could tell that she didn't have much left in her. The only thing that was keeping her going was the fact that she thought Chris was alive; she longed to be with him. Mike needed her to hang on for just one more day. He knew that the second Presidential Address was going to take place that evening at seven o'clock-that was their window of opportunity. It would take most of the day to map out the plan.

The time was four o'clock, only an hour and a half before they would need to leave. Mike had been working diligently on the plan for hours and felt confident about its potential for success. Jessica had just finished a shower and it was Laura's turn. Mike slipped in quickly to use the restroom since Laura's said she was going to take a long bath.

As Mike sat back down to continue his plan, he felt Jessica massaging his neck. It felt so good! His tension had been building for months…no, years. He longed so much for their past lives; happiness, bliss, contentment. At that moment, he was feeling tingly all over. It wasn't a professional massage; she wanted something else…he did too.

"You have been working so hard Mike," she whispered in his ear, then kissing his neck. "I miss you. We haven't been together in months. She'll be in there for a while…come on," she beckoned, now massaging his chest from behind. He couldn't resist…he wanted her too. The timing of it couldn't have been worse, but Mike felt that they both had a sense that this could be the last time they would be together-it might have been.

They made love. As they laid there afterwards, Mike felt many emotions going through his body. He was content yet felt miserable.

Mike was fearless yet felt scared. He was confident yet felt uncertain. One thing that he was certain of was that they needed to get to The White House. It was all about to go down.

As they drove to their destination, they could see a lot of people in the streets. The government had taken over all radio waves and directions were heard on every radio station...all the same. Every station was in the same voice, giving directions to the public about what to do. The monotone voice spoke, "All people, please return to your homes...everything is under control. The government has a plan in place that will work, but only if all people return to your homes and follow the instructions."

No station had music; not yet. Mike remembered that the Brian told him that the music wouldn't return until after *Sun Death*. Then the radio would be controlled by the government as a way to help appease the dying public.

Every few blocks they saw a Hummer with a loudspeaker on the roof. They were projecting the same directions as on the radio, but the people weren't listening. They weren't rioting in Washington, not yet. But as they got closer to The White House, the crowds grew larger and they were flocking towards The President's home. Mike needed a big mob for his plan to work.

As they got a few blocks from The White House, the crowds were too large for them to continue driving. There was obviously law enforcement in the area as empty police cars were everywhere; seeping tear gas cans laid sporadically around the streets. The conditions were helping the crowd, as the winds were gusty, maybe twenty-five miles per hour, and dissipated the tear gas quicker than it could form a significant cloud. The three of them were going to have their work cut out for them with this crowd; it seemed to have organization.

After Mike parked the car, they continued on foot. They could see a man, standing on the roof of a police car, shouting to everyone. He was a tall, lanky black man with short hair, graying above his ears. He had a bullhorn in his hand and his voice was loud and clear.

"Alright, people!" he shouted, "Keep moving toward The White House! The only way we're going to get answers is from the man himself! Don't fear the police, they're outnumbered!"

The crowd appeared to be a mix of all races. It wasn't predominantly black or white. The people were coming out of their homes to get some answers. Mike approached the man.

"Excuse me sir!" Mike was trying to get a word in as he the man yelled to the crowd, "Excuse me!" he tugged at the man's pant leg.

"Yes," the man turned the bullhorn off and peered down at Mike, "what can I do for you?" he said impatiently.

"Look, are you leading this group?" Mike asked.

"I'm trying to…why?" the man was suspicious of Mike's intentions.

"If I could have a minute of your time, I think we could work together. I have some information to share with you about this that will blow your mind!"

"Like what?" he said in a distrustful tone.

"I'd prefer to talk to you in a more quiet place." People were bumping into Mike as they spoke.

"Okay," the man pointed, "let's go over there, that deli is abandoned."

As they approached the deli, there was a closed sign on the door; a neon sign read "Corrasco's Deli." A small square of glass was broken to the left of the door and someone had unlocked it. As they walked in, it looked as though it was open for business. It had probably been abandoned in the last twenty-four hours. The man walked behind the counter.

"Would you like some coffee?" he asked the three of them.

"No thanks," Mike and Jessica answered.

"Yes, I would like some," Laura said.

"Well, this is my office! The owners left this morning when the crowd started forming. Never thought I would be an entrepreneur," he laughed, "here you go," handing the cup to Laura, "there's cream and sugar on the table." He sat across from Mike, "I guess we should introduce ourselves, I'm Shaun," he extended his hand.

"I'm Mike Collins, and this is my wife, Jessica. And that's Laura."

They all exchanged nodding of the heads.

"Alright, Mike, what's this information you have?" Shaun said impatiently.

"Well, I have been working for the government for over a decade and…"

"Wait a second. You're that guy on the news! The one they're looking for! You had that shootout at The White house the other day! And you also led police on that manhunt last month!"

"Yeah, that's me. But I did it for a reason. Look…"

"I'm not here to judge you sir. He'll do that," Shaun pointed up to the ceiling, "and very soon. It's Judgment Day!"

"What do you mean?" Mike wondered what the man knew.

"Come on, you've heard of Judgment Day! The world is ending! This is what all of us have been waiting for!" Shaun spoke in a very loud tone and Mike wondered if he even needed a bullhorn.

"You're talking about God, right?" Mike was hoping he didn't sound ignorant.

"Of course! What else is there?" Shaun laughed.

"A lot actually," Jessica interjected. Then she giggled and shook her head, still in disbelief as to what was going on.

"Yeah…a lot," Laura muttered in a depressed tone.

"What are you guys talking about?"

"What I am about to tell you is highly classified and we have to be cautious as to how we exploit it with what's going on. I guess it being classified doesn't mean shit since most of humanity is supposed to perish."

"What are you saying? That this isn't spiritual? That this has something to do with the government?" Shaun stood up.

"Exactly! It's scientific. I'm not spiritual…so maybe it could be God's version of Judgment Day…I don't know! All I know is that I want to share some information with you and I think we can use it to help both of us."

"Okay…" Shaun said with skepticism. He sat down again.

"Well, as I was saying, I have been working with the government for over a decade on top-secret projects and I uncovered *Sun Death* years ago."

"*Sun Death*?"

"Yes, you know, the sun being hit by the white dwarf star?"

"I knew that…but The President said they just found out about this?" Shaun stood up again.

"He lied. They've known about this for decades, but here's the catch. They really don't think mankind can survive this...they're snowballing us into thinking we can so they can escape."

"Escape to where?"

"To a space station they've been building since the sixties!"

"So we're all going to die down here?" reality was setting in on Shaun; he started pacing back and forth. He had accepted his fate on God's terms, but now that science had a hand in his demise, things were different.

"No we're not! I have a plan...but we need help. From someone like you."

Mike went on to explain exactly how they were going to survive and what he needed Shaun, Jessica and Laura to do. He had to cover it quickly, as time was running out. It was only twenty minutes until The President would address the world again.

As they exited the diner, Shaun and Laura headed off in different directions. Mike grabbed Jessica and gave her a long hug and a quick kiss.

"Now you be careful!" Mike held her chin as he talked to her. "This could be dangerous. Stick to the plan and everything should be alright. Got it?"

"Got it. You be careful too! You're the one we have to worry about!"

"Don't worry about me...I love you!" he hugged her again.

"I love you too!"

Mike could already hear Shaun on the bullhorn. If the plan was going to work, Shaun would have to get the crowd riled up. And he was just the type of person who could do it.

"Alright people! The President of the United States is going to address us in about ten minutes! I need everyone to move over to The White House! I have some very important news to share with you after his address...come on! Let's go! It's only a few blocks away!" the crowd wasn't listening to Shaun. They were moving too slow.

Mike could see that Shaun's piece of the plan wasn't working fast enough. Mike had to start moving toward The White House. He jogged ahead of the crowd. He found it strange that the police weren't trying to dispel the crowd. There weren't many police or military personnel around the crowd at all. As he got closer toward his destination, Mike could see where they all were-guarding The White House.

Mike could see that there were already several hundred people grouped together outside the nation's capital. The problem was that there were also several hundred police and military personnel protecting it. Mike was counting on Shaun to get the rest of the crowd over to him. Mike needed the crowd to outnumber the police and military personnel significantly; they needed to intimidate the men and women guarding The President. At least they thought The President was in there. Shaun was bringing between five hundred and a thousand more people, but it would be a while until they got to Mike.

The directions on the loudspeakers could be heard announcing that The President would address the nation in two minutes. Several of the Hummer's pulled up in front of the crowd and the voice could be heard loudly.

"Good evening ladies and gentlemen across our great country and the world…I would like to start out this evening by addressing how some people around the world are reacting to this situation. I have received reports that people are rioting across the globe, and it is making the process of preparing for the weather conditions to come, much more difficult. As I speak to you from the Oval Office, hundreds of people are forming outside at this very moment. Therefore, I have no other alternative, but to impose an immediate curfew on all residents of this great nation," the crowd started booing and the people were looking at one another as if they didn't know what to do. "This is being implemented for the safety of our citizens and all local, state and federal law enforcement personnel. These men and women are serving their country in order to make this unfortunate situation as comfortable as possible for all of us. I have also heard that many people across our country, and the globe, are taking this situation and turning it into a much larger flight of the imagination-this is not Judgment Day! I repeat…this is not the end of the world! This will be a blackout that may, or may not be, permanent. We have top scientists all over the world working feverishly on determining just that. But we must have peace and serenity across this great world in order for us to get two very important things accomplished. First we have to assess if this is temporary or permanent; then we have to decide what our plan of action will be. We have basic plans in place for both, but the chaos forming is making it much more difficult for them to be attained. If the people of the United States listen to the directions given to them, all of you can make it through this without any problems. Yes, there are a few things that have happened that we did not anticipate. Currently we have several manufacturers that have stepped up production on many of the supplies needed to appease all Americans; many of them at two hundred percent or more! But what we need is for the people of this great land to proceed in a civilized manner. Unfortunately a small number of people have acted inappropriately, which has forced me to impose this curfew…which is effective immediately! Any person found to be out in public will be arrested on site. The government will take care of ensuring each person, and family, has adequate supplies necessary for this situation. The collision with the sun will take place in about thirty minutes. I need everyone to stay calm. Do not panic! I repeat, do not panic! If we all work together, we can overcome this hurdle. Our founding fathers came to America hundreds of years ago and overcame huge obstacles in order to accomplish their goals. Today we are being tested again. Our will is being tested, as well as our resolve and determination to survive! Our nation has endured other difficult situations, and I have complete confidence in what the American people can do. I also have complete confidence in the rest of the world being able to endure this. If we all stay calm, and follow the directions given to us…everything will be fine. I will continue to address the nation every twenty-four hours. Let's be strong, and God bless all of you and this great earth."

The crowd was dumfounded. People looked at one another wondering what to do now. The President sounded sincere and his directions were clear and concise; the crowd should disperse and everyone should head home and wait for directions on what to do next. Mike could see the life of the crowd slowly dying and had to do something. And now.

"People! Listen," Mike yelled several times, each time louder. Out of the corner of his eye he could see several of the guards at The White House gate talking and pointing at him. "Look! Everything isn't what it appears to be! This is a huge conspiracy…" he paused as he could see that the men in front of The White House were walking over to several soldiers. The men were talking, but their eyes were glued on Mike. The pause in Mike's shouting made it obvious to the crowd that something had Mike's attention and quickly people started looking in the same direction, then back at Mike, then back at the soldiers. "No matter what happens to me, don't believe what The President is telling you..." his fear stopped him from continuing.

A group of about ten armed soldiers and the two men, probably secret service, were quickly walking toward him. As he gazed back in the direction that Shaun was supposed to be coming, machine gun blasts exploded; Mike fell to the ground. As quickly as the guns were heard, the crowd dispersed in all directions-it was complete pandemonium. As Mike raised his head off the ground, he saw a half-dozen M-16's pointed directly at him. The men were close, maybe eight feet away. Everything was happening in slow motion and he couldn't move. Mike remembered that he had put on a bulletproof vest, but it would be no match for the military hardware that they had. Not to mention if he took a head shot, which would be very likely at that range.

"Freeze Asshole!" Mike heard and he turned his head again to where Shaun was supposed to be coming from, "hands behind your head!"

There was no Shaun. There was no large crowd of people to help Mike. He was on his own again. A few people could be seen off in the distance, two or three blocks away, but there was nothing they could do for him now. He was amidst about thirty military and police personnel. He could hear the secret service men trying to convince the police that they should give Mike to them.

"No! I'll go with the police! The suits will kill me! They're in on this too! Don't let me go with the suits!" Mike pleaded. He had picked up the nickname years ago and really didn't know why other than the obvious. They always wore suits = "suits." It was easier to say than secret service and if "suits" was mentioned in front of others, people wouldn't freak out. Heads turned when people heard the words "secret service."

"Shut the fuck up!" one of the secret service men screamed in Mike's face. "You killed my partner you son of a bitch!"

"Yeah, and you killed mine...we're even!" Mike retorted, touching his nose to the man's.

The man turned away and then slung his fist around at Mike's face, quicker than he could react. Mike was out cold.

As Mike regained consciousness, he had no idea where he was or how long he had been out. What he did know was that he was lying on the floor, hands behind his back, handcuffed. After quickly surveying the room, he could see that the two suits had gotten their way; he was inside The White House. He thought, *What in the hell am I going to do now? I hope Jessica is fine! What happened to Shaun?* The door to the room opened.

"Oh, I see you're awake now. How's your shiner?" a suit questioned sarcastically.

"That guy packs quite a punch!" Mike laughed even though he was in pain.

"Here's some water," he extended it to Mike's face.

"Poison?"

"Yeah right. You thirsty or not?"

"What are the chances of getting these off?" Mike turned halfway around exposing the handcuffs.

"We can put them in the front, but that's it. And no funny business or I'll put them back behind you!"

"Understood. How long have I been out?"

"About ten minutes." The suit swapped his handcuffs to Mike's front.

Mike looked to see what time it was, but his watch was gone.

"Where the hell is my watch?"

"I have no idea."

"That was given to me from my father…and to him, by his! I want to know where the hell it is!"

"Look, yelling at me isn't going to get you anywhere! I'll ask around, but I can't give you any promises. Maybe you lost it in the scuffle."

"What time is it?"

"About 7:45."

"She's just about here. But the boss says we can survive it. I just hope he's right."

"Survive? Not for long! Do you know anything about the sun? What's your name?" Mike had to start on him immediately.

"Ben...Ben Donaldson."

Mike extended his cuffed hands, "Nice to meet you. Mike Collins. I'm sure you knew that. The sun provides life here on earth. Without it, the planet would be a cold, dark, dead place."

"Are you're saying we're going to die?"

"Not exactly. Without the sun, yes we would die."

"Then what are you saying?" Mike had Ben's undivided attention.

"Do you know where The President is?"

"Not exactly. A couple of us have been talking though, and we think they moved him to NORAD."

"Really?"

"Yeah. That's the most logical place...just in case...you know, to play it safe."

"Say, do you know anyone who works in NORAD?" Mike questioned.

"Yeah. Why?"

"Me too. Let me prove something to you!"

"What? Look, this is ridiculous! I have work to do! I was just bringing you a drink! Do you want some or not?" Ben started walking toward the door.

"Okay. Just do one thing...trust me," Mike followed him to the door, "I'm not fucking with you! Just try and find out where The President is...I bet you can't! I bet you can't get one person on this planet to tell you that they know for sure where he is! Someone that has seen him, personally!"

"What are you saying? That The President isn't here on earth?" Ben laughed.

Mike just stood there and looked at him with the most serious look he had ever given someone.

"You're serious. They told me you were nuts, but this..." Ben looked at Mike waiting for his sincerity to stop, but it didn't. Ben stopped laughing, "Your serious?"

"Dead serious!"

Ben paused for a moment, just staring at Mike. He peered into Mike's eyes, deep in thought as to his motives. He knew Mike was dangerous and didn't want to play into a trap, but he also felt Mike was genuine in his words; he could see it in Mike's eyes.

"Hmm. I guess it wouldn't hurt to make a few phone calls."

"Please, do it! You'll be astounded with what you find!"

"We'll see," Ben said as he walked out of the room.

Mike quickly grabbed the door before Ben closed it and whispered, "Do me one favor though. Don't tell anybody we had this conversation. If the wrong person finds out, they'll kill me. Look, I'll make you a deal. If you find, without a doubt, that The President is here, then I don't care who you tell, but first find out...that's all I ask. Please, this is a matter of life and death."

"Alright, but if you're fucking with me..."

"Trust me, I'm not. My life depends on it."

"Yeah, it does," and Ben closed the door.

Mike could hear him lock the door from the outside. All that was on Mike's mind was escaping; he was a prisoner again. He looked out the window and confirmed that he was at The White House. He could see a group of people in the street, outside the entrance to The White House and there were troops guarding the fortress from the inside. The group in the street was smaller than the one that had formed when Mike was out there and likewise a much smaller group of soldiers. He strained his eyes, looking for a figure that resembled Jessica, Laura or Shaun, but it was too far away.

Mike had no way of telling what time it was. He knew this day would come, but he never prepared for it mentally. He had envisioned it happening, but not how he would feel experiencing it first hand. Mike wasn't sure how long he would be held captive or what would happen to him, but he was sure that the longer they held him, the worse his chances of staying alive. He figured that whoever was left at The White House was holding Mike until they got word from The President as to his fate.

Mike wondered how the people on *The Station* were holding up on the verge of witnessing *Sun Death*. How they felt about their friends and family members being on the planet that once flourished with life. To them, earth was about to become a cold, dark planet, uninhabitable by man. To them, it was death.

Chapter 14

The New Beginning

Mike saw two days come and go, with no visitors other than someone bringing him meals. The food wasn't bad considering he was a prisoner, but each meal was cold. For breakfast he was served scrambled eggs, sausage, some toast, an English muffin, and a cup of coffee. Lunch was just two sandwiches; and dinner, the same.

Mike was concerned that he hadn't seen Ben in those two days. He thought that the room might have been tapped and somebody overheard their conversation. If that had happened, they might have transferred Ben to another location. Another concern of Mike's was that the amount of people outside The White House had dwindled to just a few each day. He was becoming obsessed with having to know what time it was.

Mike decided to rummage through the room. There weren't any visible cameras in the room, he just had to keep it quiet. All of the furniture in the room was genuine and expensive looking…dark cherry wood. The desk he was sitting at was a huge executive desk that looked like it had been around for a half-century. He started searching through the drawers. Mike looked around the room as he searched for something; he didn't know what for, but something. On top of the desk, there was a feather pen and ink, but it was just for show. There was a clock on the wall, but it wasn't working. A picture of George Washington was also on the wall-the first President's eyes followed Mike no matter where he went in the room. Mike spoke to him, "I bet you never thought it would come to this, did you? The sun dying and the government trying to only save themselves." He found a pager in one of the drawers. He looked at the LCD and it gave him the date and time. It was September 7, 2:32 p.m.

Suddenly someone was fidgeting with the lock on the door. Mike quickly put the pager in his pocket and leaned back in the oversized burgundy executive chair. The first face he saw was Jessica's. He quickly jumped to his feet and headed towards her.

"Honey, are you okay? What are you doing here?" he grabbed her and gave her a hug. Next he saw Shaun, who looked at Mike like a son who had just let his father down on game day; they had been captured. The only people who could rescue Mike were now imprisoned with him. Mike thought *It's time to throw in the towel! This fight's over!*

"You," a soldier pointed at Mike, "go over there, on the other side of the sofa while I move their cuffs!"

"Thank you," Jessica sincerely responded.

The soldier unlocked her cuffs, turned her around and locked them in front, "Those comfortable?"

"Yes, thank you."

The soldier got up in Shaun's face, "Now when I unlock these, you're gonna behave yourself, right?"

"Yes, sir," Shaun responded. It was obvious to Mike that the two already had a rapport with one another; and not a positive one. That could explain the busted-up lip the soldier had.

"If not, Private Maxwell here," he looked at the other soldier standing at the door, is going to light you up…got it?" He had a M-16 draped over his shoulder-finger on trigger.

"Yes, sir," Shaun responded in the same tone. He was patronizing the soldier.

After they were finished, the soldiers exited the room and locked the door. Shaun sat on the sofa, leaned over, and put his head in his hands. Mike walked over to Jessica and put his arms around her.

"What happened? How did you guys get caught?"

"We were out there, trying to get the crowd pumped up and the next thing we knew, some soldiers singled us out. I guess because we were directing everyone. I don't know! Shaun punched a few soldiers...he's lucky he didn't get killed!"

"Where's Laura," Mike asked.

"We have no idea," Jessica answered.

"So what's been going on out there? Any news from The President or anything? They haven't told me anything in here. They just bring me food three times a day."

"I sure could use some right now," Shaun looked at his watch.

"They should be by soon," Mike responded, "so what's going on out there, Shaun?"

"Mike...it's crazy out there...you won't believe what's going on! You know that plan that the government had to drop leaflets all over the U.S. and for this zip code and that zip code to come out and get supplies?" Mike nodded, "It's all out the window."

"What do you mean?"

"I mean, it was all bullshit! The President had a speech last night and it's not looking good. *Sun Death* hasn't happened and they think their calculations are off or something; boy are they in for a huge surprise! But, apparently most of the U.S. has lost confidence that we can even survive this. One-third of all law enforcement and military has stopped reporting for duty. Three fourths of Americans have stopped showing up for work. Finally, they shut down the media! They were showing riots all over the place; I think once people saw it on TV, they gave up. I've talked to some people and they think that there is no chance of humanity living through this. It's been on every news report, every talk show. Everyone's predicting that this is it. Oh, and the suicide bombings..."

"What suicide bombings?" Mike stood up.

"Well...the news said that all of these terrorist cells across the country took this opportunity to come out of hiding or something.

There are bombings everywhere! Suicide, car, some guy tried to fly a Cessna into a government building in L.A. There have also been some mass suicides; some cults. And I guess a couple of Militia Groups have organized small army's and are planning something. I think the one in Michigan is pretty big…it's all crazy!"

"All of this," Mike fumbled around in his pocket and pulled out the pager, "less than a week after *Sun Death* was announced. Have you guys started to get the word out there about what's really happening…you have, right?"

Shaun and Jessica looked at each other in a puzzling manner.

"That's not what you told us to do, honey!" Jessica sternly replied.

"Yeah, but I didn't anticipate getting caught either!"

"Look," Shaun jumped in, "our main priority was to get you out of here! We tried to get the crowd going, and it was starting to work, then they got us," Shaun looked at his watch again. "I think we may have a chance of getting out of here. When they were grabbing me, I told a friend to do the same thing tomorrow, at the same time."

"Do what?" Mike's face showed hope.

"Well, the other day…no yesterday…I'm losing track. Anyways, the other day we started a major riot down on the south side of town. This was a diversion for what we were really doing."

"Yeah, I saw a bunch of the soldiers leaving the front lawn. I was wondering what happened," Mike remembered.

"Yeah, we had several hundred people down there trashing the police station, lighting fires. We did it to get the soldiers away from here and it worked. They're going to do it again tomorrow at noon."

"That's our chance to get out of here!" Mike was excited, "We have to let the country and the world know…hey, how's the rest of the world dealing with this?"

"Oh, you're going to love this," Jessica said as she looked at Shaun, "tell him."

"What?" it was killing Mike.

"Well, the world is in utter chaos. After seeing people in our country freak out, the rest of the world did the same. Word leaked out that the heat and radiation was going to hit the Eastern Hemisphere and they've gone crazy! A few wars have started. Let's see…China went into Taiwan, North and South Korea are going at it, and India and Pakistan are on the verge of Nuclear War again. Oh yeah, the best one is that most of the Arab countries are banning against Israel. The U.S. and Britain are the only countries helping to defend them, but the U.S. military is in disarray. Before they shut off the media, there were some crazy reports out there. Mutiny, and all kinds of weird things…it's crazy! I think even if the world does survive this, it's going to be a disaster. Hell, this could be the start of World War III!"

Mike sat down on the couch; he was depressed. He couldn't help but think that he could have prevented all of the mayhem across the globe; the innocent people dying. He still wanted to wake up from this nightmare…it was surreal. Beating himself up wouldn't change anything…he had to stop it. Stop it now. He remembered when Brian told him that people's lives were in Mike's hands-that was never truer than it was now. He had to act quickly.

Mike walked over to the window. He could see that the crowd outside was growing; it was considerably larger than before. Off in the distance, Mike could see the top half of a man sticking out of the roof of a car. It appeared to be a black man and he was piercing through the sunroof, trying to pump up the crowd. Hundreds of people were moving toward the already large group, which Mike figured had to be between one and two thousand.

"Shaun, come here!" Mike exclaimed, pointing out the window.

"What is it?" Shaun walked over to the window.

"See that guy…way over there, behind the crowd? The one sticking out of the sun roof, with a bull horn?"

"Yeah, that's my man, Marty! Looks like he's a little early, but maybe something happened!"

"What are we going to do?" someone yelled in the hallway outside their room.

"Call the General! We need more troops! They took most of them to the south side of town to take care of that riot! Hurry!" the voice was distressed.

Mike walked over and put his ear up to the door, straining to hear anything, but the voices faded. He walked back over to the window and could see the crowd growing. There were only several dozen police and military personnel on the opposite side of the fence from the crowd. They were no match for the mob preparing to overtake the fortress. Many of the people had sticks, bats, tire irons, and other objects in their hands; they appeared ready to do something. Again, they could see Marty. The car he was in was driving back and forth, apparently in an attempt to rile up the crowd. Suddenly the door to the room opened. It was Ben.

"Mike, there isn't much time! They're coming up here to kill all of you!" Ben slammed the door behind him and locked it.

"Who?" Mike questioned.

"Some soldiers! I guess they just got the call from The President! I don't think we'll have time to get out of here! Here, give me a hand." Ben started sliding a desk over in front of the door. Next, they put a smaller desk on top of it to form a barricade for what was to come. Ben sat down behind the barricade; he looked exhausted.

"You alright?" Mike asked.

"I don't know. This is just too much!" he started to open a duffle bag.

"What happened?"

"It's just like you said. I made about ten phone calls and no one could tell me where The President was. And I know some people! Then I talked to this guy that went to the Academy with me, we've been buddies forever. He told me that he had heard some rumors about The President going up into space. And that the government thought we weren't going to be able to survive this."

"I told you."

"So what the hell is going on?" Ben demanded. He pulled out a gas mask and tossed it to Jessica, "Here, you might need this. Go on Mike."

"He left us. They could have saved about six hundred more people, but he decided not to," Mike explained as Ben handed a mask to Shaun.

"Where'd they go?"

"Up to a space station."

"Like a space ship?" Ben looked confused. He lastly handed a mask to Mike.

"Exactly. They've been building it for decades."

"They've known about this for decades?" Ben got up and looked out the window. He knelt down and started pulling weapons out of his bag.

"Yup, since the early sixties," Mike acknowledged.

Suddenly, it happened. Shots rang out from in front of The White House. All four of them rushed to the window to see what melee was underway. Hundreds of people were scaling the fence as soldiers tried to pick them off one at a time, but it was futile. The soldiers had no confidence, they were backpedaling and there weren't enough of them. Suddenly Mike saw a Fed Ex truck barrel through the main gate. A dozen or so people came pouring out of the truck as well as through the main entrance. The soldiers defending the fortress were overpowered swiftly. They were no match for the crowd stampeding toward The White House. There was smoke in the air, most likely tear gas, but it wasn't enough. Commotion was heard in the hallway.

"Holy shit! I'm not sure what they're doing, but I think if those soldiers don't kill us, the crowd might," Ben started handing guns to each of them, "Look, they're pouring in! I hope you guys know how to use these."

"Are you kidding," Jessica responded and looked to Mike, "being married to one of the FBI's most wanted...you have to."

"I think we'll be alright," Mike pointed out the window, "see that man coming in the gate," Ben was looking into the crowd, "the car with the man sticking out of the sun roof," Ben focused, "That's Shaun's friend. They're here to save us!"

"You know him?" Ben looked to Shaun.

"Yeah, he's going to get us out of this shithole!"

"Let us in!" they heard with a bang on the door. Ben put his index finger over his lips for them to keep quiet. "Now! Open the door!" Ben recognized the voice as one of the men he reported to. It was Dan, his sergeant.

"So you can do what?" Ben yelled back. Then he whispered to Mike and the others, "get down." Ben sat with his back to the desks stacked against the door, hoping to help reinforce the barricade. Mike joined him and told Jessica to move to the other side of the room and get down. Shaun knelt behind another desk for cover.

The men outside the room were trying to bust down the door. Ben popped his head up and pointed his 9mm towards the door, but aimed it toward the wall above the door. He squeezed off three warning shots. Everything got quiet.

"Get the hell out of here!" Ben yelled.

"Okay, we can do this the hard way!" the voice responded.

Shots rang out again, only this time they came from the hallway. The bullets pierced through the door and flew over Mike and Ben. It was obviously a machine gun, probably a M-16. Splinters of wood flew over them as they held their position bracing the desks against the door. Mike could see Jessica, who had good cover and was out of the path of the bullets. Shaun also. After the men emptied their clip, Ben knew they had a few seconds to respond. Ben opened fire at the door, then Mike joined in. They emptied their magazine and then they heard more commotion in the hallway. It sounded like some of the crowd had made it to them.

"Hold your fire in there!" a voice yelled from the hallway.

Mike and Ben popped their heads up. Movement could be seen in the hallway through the bullet-riddled door. The once solid, three inch thick, cherry door looked ready to crumble to the floor. Jessica and Shaun didn't move an inch.

"Who's out there?" Mike yelled.

"My name's Todd. Is there a Shaun or a Mike in there?"

"Maybe, who wants to know?" Mike yelled back.

Then another voice was heard, "Marty! It's me, Marty!"

"That's him!" Shaun got up from behind the desk that sheltered him. Jessica popped up and they all started moving the desks. Everyone but Mike. He sat down; his heart was pounding like it never had before. It was so dreamlike. He felt buzzed from everything that had transpired. Ears ringing, his mind quickly relived the last year. *Government conspiracy, shootout in The White House, imprisonment, death, destruction. Hollywood couldn't have produced a better story* he thought.

"Honey, are you alright?" Jessica sat down next to him.

He was in a daze and just shook his head back and forth.

"What is it?" she had her hand on his shoulder.

"All of this...all of this could have been avoided...if, if I could have let the world know what's really going on."

"Honey, everything's going to be okay."

"No, people have died! But we're going to fix this mess," Mike was regaining his focus; he stood up, "Shaun, did you mention it to Marty about the news crew?"

"Yeah, but let me talk to him and make sure they're coming."

Mike wasn't sure of what had transpired during the last few minutes; it was a blur. The desks were moved, the door was open and a few people could be seen walking back and forth in the hallway. Hopefully they were in a safe zone now. Mike had work to do.

As Mike walked out of the room, he saw blood in the hallway. Presumably from the men shooting at them through the doors. Mike hated death, but he had to focus on the job at hand. As they walked down the hallway, hundreds of people could be seen out on The White House lawn. They were rallying together...they were getting organized. Surely law enforcement, or the military, would be there soon since they thought The President was still in the building they had just overtaken.

Mike saw two young-looking soldiers walking towards him in the hallway. They were talking and Mike was listening to their words as they got closer.

"Yeah, and just when the soldier downstairs grabbed the radio, I'm sure he was going to warn someone about us taking over The White House, I blew him away! This shotgun almost blew his head clean off! It was great!" then he laughed and the other joined in.

Mike grabbed the boy and threw him against the wall, "You son of a bitch! You think it's funny to kill one of our own? These men were serving our country! They were just doing their jobs! They probably have a wife and kids at home!" he pulled him a few inches away from the wall and then slammed him up against it again. The soldier's friend started to step in and Shaun put his hand on the man's chest. Mike put his 9mm against the kid's temple. "Huh? You think its funny?" the makeshift soldier was eighteen at the oldest and had no comprehension of the significance of death-the meaning of life. Mike just stared at him for a few seconds, putting the fear of God into him. He let him go and Mike continued down the hallway. The kids ran the other way.

It was 6:30 p.m. and the timing of their rescue couldn't have been more perfect; it was just about time for The President to address the world again. Mike had a half an hour to prepare for his chance to save lives; his chance to make things right. They made their way to the Oval Office and Mike sat down at The President's desk, suddenly feeling the magnitude of everything that had transpired. He had many emotions going through his body, but it was time to be strong. This was his only chance to make things right. He started jotting down what he wanted to say to the American public…to the world.

The plan was for a news crew to set up their camera equipment in the Oval Office and tap into The President's speech. He wanted to let The President start the speech and Mike would end it. He would show the public that The President had abandoned the people on earth and left them to die. Shaun assured Mike that the technician at the television station could hack into the signal.

"Hello, are you Mike Collins?" a slim, beautiful lady walked into the Oval Office.

"Yes. And you are?" Mike stood up and extended his hand.

"Sherry, Sherry White."

"Nice to meet you."

Jessica had been looking out the window, but her attention was on the model-like brunette who was shaking her husbands hand-shaking it for too long, in her opinion. The woman was more beautiful than Jessica, and any man who said he wasn't attracted to her, was lying. Jessica looked her up and down, and then looked at Mike; they were flirting. She wasn't the jealous type, but with everything that had been happening, she was a little insecure.

"Hello," Jessica said as she walked toward the woman, "I'm his wife, Jessica," she extended her hand. They exchanged hands and the atmosphere between Mike and Sherry changed. That was Jessica's goal.

The rest of the news crew entered and began setting up all of the equipment. When they were finished, it looked like a Hollywood studio. There were three different cameras that would be on Mike; four microphones to speak into. There would be eight people working behind the scenes. He wasn't sure if he could do it. He wasn't a shy person, but at the same time, he wasn't a great public speaker. In college, he dreaded the speech classes. He convinced himself that he was only talking to three cameras and a dozen or so people that would be in the room-he would picture them all naked.

The President began to address the world. As the television showed The President, he was sitting in a replica of the room Mike was in. Mike looked at the television, then quickly surveyed the room…it was perfect.

"Good evening, ladies and gentlemen. I would like to take this opportunity to touch base with you on the status of our preparations for dealing with the current situation. Believe it, or not, I am actually lacking in the proper supplies to deal with this myself," he said it so believably, it was sick, "but we are making progress. I do have a request for the American public: we have to get back to work in order for this to be successful. As you can see," the video switched to footage of some rioting, "some people are hindering the process by looting and rioting. I assure you that these mobs will be curtailed and brought to justice. People, we are better than this! We have to be strong. We have work to do. Now...the conditions are not nearly as dire as we had predicted. In fact, the dwarf hasn't struck the sun yet; we are currently looking into why the collision has not transpired yet." When he said that, Mike knew exactly why it hadn't happened yet.

"Can we cut-in now?" Mike asked Sherry.

She looked over to the technician who was sitting in front of a laptop. He looked back to her, then at the computer, then back at Sherry and nodded.

"Sure Mike. You let me know when. Then I'll count down from five."

"Let's do it," Mike said with confidence.

She looked at everyone and they all nodded with assurance that they were ready for action. The President was still talking, but it was time for Mike to go to work. She held her hand up and then counted down with her fingers.

Mike was startled. He could see his own face on the television monitors instead of The President's. He had to speak, but he hesitated.

"Um...hello American people, and the world. Hopefully there are hundreds of millions of you watching, or listening tonight..."

Back on *The Station*-things were getting tense.

Chapter 15

Payback

"What the fuck is going on?" The Vice-President yelled.

"Yes, what's going on," The President stood up from his desk in the replica office.

They could see the face of Mike Collins on the television screen. Mike was sitting in the Oval Office; the same one that The President was supposed to be in-Mike was addressing the nation...addressing the world.

"How the hell is he there? Call the White House! Somebody do something!" The President was furious. Five men and a woman sprinted out of the room.

The President's top aid walked over to him, "Sir, it's going to be alright. I'm sure we can shut him down quickly," she was trying to cut the tension. She wasn't very believable.

Back on earth.

"As you can see, I am in the Oval Office, not The President. This is the real Oval Office. What I'm about to tell you is both incredible and far-fetched, and to some, absurd, but it's true. The President was speaking to you from a phony Oval Office up in space. Yes, up in space. But the most important thing that I need to tell you is that humanity is not going to perish! I know millions of people across the globe have stopped going to work, and stopped being productive. Some have taken to crime and others gone to war. I know that the word has gotten out there that we are all going to die. We are not going to die! I repeat, we are not going to die! Yes, if the dwarf star was to collide with the sun, it would be devastating; we would die. But it's not going to. Let me back up a bit, and excuse my speech. I didn't have time to write it out, and I don't have political advisers, or speech advisors, I'm just talking to you. I'm talking to you from one human being to billions of others out there. I guess I should tell you who I am. My name is Mike Collins and I have been employed with the government for decades. I am a scientist and many of you in the states may recognize me from the manhunt when I was falsely accused of several crimes, including murder. Anyways, I'm going to cut to the chase. Three scientists before me had confirmed that the white dwarf was going to collide with the sun. Not a direct collision, but enough to cause the sun to eventually extinguish. Before dying, the sun would release as much heat and radioactivity in one day as it normally would in one hundred million years causing the end of humanity. During my findings, I also uncovered that the government has known about this since the Roswell, New Mexico incident in 1955. Extra-terrestrials did come to earth, but they came to warn us of *Sun Death* and give us technology to escape from earth…"

Back on The Station.

"Why the hell isn't someone shooting him. Get some plane to drop an bomb on the damn thing," The Vice-President yelled.

"Sir, unfortunately that's not possible. Someone has hacked into our satellite links to earth and we are cut off from contacting anyone down there."

"Bullshit! If somebody hacked in, have somebody hack into them! What the hell did we bring all those computer guru fuckers up here for?"

"Yes, Sir."

Richard just stood there, staring at the television thinking, *I knew I should have killed that son of a bitch.*

Back on Earth.

"Of course, when those extra-terrestrials came to earth, we shot down their aircraft and they were killed. But the technology they helped us uncover was phenomenal. It put us decades ahead in ground, air, and space travel. Since the 1960's we have been building a space station intended to house one thousand people and save them from *Sun Death.* The U.S. Government had a plan! A plan to save one thousand people from perishing here on earth! There wasn't enough time to save billions. So what this President did was decide that he didn't want to chance having all one thousand people on board. Right now, there are only about four hundred people up there, on *The Station.* And why? Why would he only save four hundred, when he could save one thousand? It was selfishness. I want it to be known that these people are some of the most corrupt individuals on this planet. The President evacuated four hundred *Chosen* individuals of which over three hundred and fifty were chosen by him. Let me get back to the sun, I don't know how long I have before they try to shut me off. I want everyone out there watching and listening to know that the world is not going to end. I am an expert on the sun and trust me...the dwarf has missed the sun. By my calculations, humanity has nothing to worry about. I know many of you, out there, have done things, some illegal, some immoral, because you thought the end of humanity was near. We need everyone to return to your regular life immediately! Everyone return home! We need all law enforcement and military personnel to return to duty immediately! This includes all people called up by The President for active duty. We need to get this situation under control and anybody who is caught doing anything illegal will be prosecuted to the fullest extent of the law!"

Mike looked over the cameraman, there were people yelling in the hallway. Someone came into the room, "Someone's coming. Looks like armored vehicles!"

Mike peered back into the lens, "Ladies and Gentlemen...I have to go now. Remember what I said, the world is not going to end and get back to normalcy in your lives. I will broadcast as soon as possible. Thank you and God bless." The transmission ended.

"Sir, there are armored vehicles and soldiers coming down the street toward us! What should we do?" a young soldier yelled to them; he was petrified.

Mike walked down the hallway and out onto a balcony. He walked out expecting to see one or two jeeps or hummers coming, but he was flabbergasted at what he saw. There had to be ten tanks, five Armored Personnel Carriers, and several hundred soldiers on foot, all fully armed for warfare; they were surrounding The White House.

"Everyone, get into position! Take cover!" Shaun yelled through a bullhorn. He was at Mike's side.

Suddenly Mike grabbed the bullhorn and yelled, "Everyone stand down! Take cover, but nobody shoots unless shot at first! Nobody make a move until I say!" Mike turned and started to walk back inside.

Mike stopped as the sound of helicopters was heard. He walked out to the end of the balcony again. The sound was ricocheting and reverberating so the direction couldn't be discerned. Then from behind him, four Apache helicopters skimmed over The White House. One went left, one right. Another kept going straight and the last stopped, slowly turned around, facing Mike and The White House.

"Oh shit!" Shaun said as he slowly backpedaled into the house.

"This isn't good!" Mike was frozen. The gun turrent from the Apache was pointed directly at Mike and the helicopter was at the same height as him. If they opened fire, the bullets would tear Mike in half. Mike turned his head slowly to look for Shaun; he was gone.

The helicopter slowly descended to the earth and as it went lower than the level of the balcony, Mike finally took a breath. Shaun reappeared on the balcony, back at Mike's side. Mike looked at him like, *Thanks for leaving me out here all alone, asshole!*

"What man...I had your back," Shaun had a guilty look on his face.

"Yeah, you had the back door, asshole."

The other Apache's started circling The White House, probably a mile, or so, away. A fifth helicopter appeared; it was much larger and it also landed on The White House lawn and shut down its engines. As they looked over the edge of the balcony, the door of the helicopter opened and six armed soldiers jumped out. Next, an officer, decorated in medals and a rainbow of ribbons, exited. He looked up at Mike, nodded as if he knew him, and walked toward The White House. The decorated soldier entered and Mike headed toward the stairs.

"Good evening, sir," Mike extended his hand.

"Please, don't call me that. It's General Schmidt. If anything, I should be calling you that," they exchanged hands and Mike laughed at his comment.

"Yeah, right. I'm Mike Collins, I'm sure you already knew that. Lets head down to the Oval Office," Mike led the way.

"Really. You're the most popular person on the planet right now!" the General said.

Mike chuckled again. Even the thought of it was dim-witted to him. After laughing, he paused for a moment to reflect on the General's comment. He realized that what the General said probably had some merit to it. Mike suddenly realized the magnitude of what he had accomplished over the last few hours. He had saved the world. They entered the office and General Schmidt closed the door.

"Sir, we are here to serve you. To defend this fortress against any enemies, foreign or domestic that may try an assault. Anything that may try to compromise your position."

"My position?" Mike was confused.

"The new Commander-in-Chief is in route and he wants you to be part of his Cabinet," the General quickly responded.

"You're kidding!"

"No, sir," the General wasn't cracking a smile. The video cameras were still set up in the room and for an instant the idea of being on one of those shows, with the hidden camera, crossed Mike's mind. "Sir, I have talked to several people on the way over here. A couple of Governors, two Mayors, and the three highest military people in the country, not including myself. Sir, the only people left are politicians…one's that couldn't cut it…one's that sit on the House of Representatives or some other committee or branch of government. We need a person to assist Frank who has values and whose mind hasn't been brainwashed with all of the political bullshit! Someone like you!"

"Frank?" Mike had no idea who he was referring to.

"Frank Anderson," the General responded.

"The head of the FBI?"

"Yeah. He's the highest ranking government official on the planet right now."

"I don't have what it takes to advise The President."

"Look at what you've done," the General walked to the window and pointed outside, "You're a survivor...a man of courage...a leader! I've known about *Sun Death* for years and your study too. I watched Dr. Sukami while he was on the project also. I know what they did to you, and your family, and what you've been through. You can do it!"

"Yeah, but help lead a whole country? We have so much work to do now. We have to rebuild. And what about The President and the others up there?"

"Fuck'em. As far as I'm concerned, they can go find a new planet to corrupt."

"Yeah, we don't need people like that on earth. Hey, did they kill Sukami? I was told he was in a better place."

"Well, the poor son of a bitch is in a worse place now! He's stuck up there with the most corrupt people in the universe!"

Back on *The Station*.

The President and Vice-President peered out the window toward earth. Half of it was in sunlight, the rest in darkness. They had been double crossed by the man they had trusted on the most important project ever conceived by man. A project to save humanity...no, a project to save the government.

"Have they confirmed that the dwarf missed the sun?" The President asked The Vice-President.

"Not yet. What do you want to do now, Mr. President?"

"I'm not sure. I don't think there's any chance of us going back...do you?"

"I doubt it," The Vice-President responded.

"We have to get in contact with the General…that's our only chance."

"General Schmidt?"

"Hell no…that bastard hates me! General Sterling."

"Oh," The Vice-President acknowledged.

"Yeah. I left him in charge. He's our only chance of getting back."

"Do you really want to go back, Mr. President? Back to all of the crime…all the bullshit? All of the crazy people on that planet? Humans have really fucked up that place! We're safer up here. Look at what we have here…it's easy!"

"I don't know…I'll sleep on it," The President responded.

"Mr. President," The Secretary of Defense entered the room, "Mr. Collins was correct…the dwarf has missed the sun!"

"So we went through all of this and it's not even going to hit it?" The President yelled, "That son of a bitch! Mike knew it all along!" he walked over to a large window; he gazed down at earth.

The President stared down at the country he used to lead. A country lit up…still alive.

Back on earth.

Mike stood on the balcony of The White House, peering up into the clear, blue sky. Staring into the heavens, thinking of The President and the people on *The Station*. Mike had the same feelings toward *The Chosen* individuals up in space as The President did toward the people on earth. He thought, *The people on earth are much better off without those people…we're safer.* Then he reflected on everything that had happened over the previous ten years. He thought of Billy and his unborn daughter that would never live; tears streamed down his face.

"That's for Billy and his sister," he said under his breath, "that's for them."

About the Author

Robert Michael was born in La Jolla, California in 1971. After spending twenty years living in California, he moved to Michigan where he continued studying Business Administration and Marketing. Robert has been a Retail Manager since 1995, but has always had creative ideas brewing inside his mind. In the new Millennium, he has used this creativity to get several business ventures started as well as write "Sun Death." He resides in the Phoenix, Arizona area with his wife, Erika, and two son's, Justin, Jr. and Hunter.

www.ingramcontent.com/pod-product-compliance
Lightning Source LLC
Chambersburg PA
CBHW030322290526
45785CB00001B/478